MW01293154

Peter
God Bless,
Jeanne

Berkeley Street Theatre

The House of Prisca and Aquila

Our mission at the House of Prisca and Aquila is to produce quality books that expound accurately the word of God to empower women and men to minister together in a multicultural church. Our writers have a positive view of the Bible as God's revelation that affects both thoughts and words, so it is plenary, historically accurate, and consistent in itself, fully reliable, and authoritative as God's revelation. Because God is true, God's revelation is true, inclusive to men and women and speaking to a multicultural church, wherein all the diversity of the church is represented within the parameters of egalitarianism and inerrancy.

The word of God is what we are expounding, thereby empowering women and men to minister together in all levels of the church and home. The reason we say women and men together is because that is the model of Prisca and Aquila, ministering together to another member of the church—Apollos: "Having heard Apollos, Priscilla and Aquila took him aside and more accurately expounded to him the Way of God" (Acts 18:26). True exposition, like true religion, is by no means boring—it is fascinating. Books that reveal and expound God's true nature "burn within us" as they elucidate the Scripture and apply it to our lives.

This was the experience of the disciples who heard Jesus on the road to Emmaus: "Were not our hearts burning while Jesus was talking to us on the road, while he was opening the scriptures to us?" (Luke 24:32). We are hoping to create the classics of tomorrow, significant and accessible trade and academic books that "burn within us."

Our "house" is like the home to which Prisca and Aquila no doubt brought Apollos as they took him aside. It is like the home in Emmaus where Jesus stopped to break bread and reveal his presence. It is like the house built on the rock of obedience to Jesus (Matt 7:24). Our "house," as a euphemism for our publishing team, is a home where truth is shared and Jesus' Spirit breaks bread with us, nourishing all of us with his bounty of truth.

We are delighted to work together with Wipf and Stock in this series and welcome submissions on a wide variety of topics from an egalitarian, inerrantist global perspective.

For more information, see our Web site:

https://sites.google.com/site/houseofpriscaandaquila/.

Berkeley Street Theatre

How Improvisation and Street Theater Emerged as
a Christian Outreach to the Culture of the Time

Edited by
JEANNE C. DEFAZIO

Foreword by
DAVID W. GILL

Afterword by
WILLIAM DAVID
SPENCER

WIPF & STOCK · Eugene, Oregon

BERKELEY STREET THEATRE
How Improvisation and Street Theater Emerged as a
Christian Outreach to the Culture of the Time

House of Prisca and Aquila Series

Wipf & Stock
An Imprint of Wipf and Stock Publishers
199 W. 8th Ave., Suite 3
Eugene, OR 97401

www.wipfandstock.com

PAPERBACK ISBN: 978-1-5326-0047-0
HARDCOVER ISBN: 978-1-5326-0049-4
EBOOK ISBN: 978-1-5326-0048-7

Manufactured in the U.S.A.

By the Same Authors

Father James Bernstein:

Discovering the Prophesies of Christ

A Family Affair (Subtitled: *Why the Orthodox Church Practices Closed Communion*)

Heaven and Hell: The Divine Fire of God's Love

Surprised by Christ: My Journey from Judaism to Orthodoxy

The Original Christian Gospel

The Orthodox Study Bible (Contributor)

Orthodoxy: Jewish and Christian

A Second Look at the Second Coming (Introduction)

Which Came First: The Church or the New Testament?

Jeanne C. DeFazio:

Creative Ways to Build Christian Community (ed. with John P. Lathrop)

How to Have an Attitude of Gratitude on the Night Shift (with Teresa Flowers)

Redeeming the Screens (ed. with William David Spencer)

Olga Soler:

Apocalypse of Youth (Artist Harriet Nesbitt as told to Olga Soler)

Epistle to the Magadalenes

Tough Inspirations from the Weeping Prophet (preface: Kevin Kirkpatrick)

William David Spencer:

Name in the Papers (A Novel)

Mysterium and Mystery: The Clerical Crime Novel

Dread Jesus

Wrestling Two Worlds (A Young Adult Novel)

God through the Looking Glass: Glimpses from the Arts
   (ed. with A.B. Spencer)

Marriage at the Crossroads: Couples in Conversation about
   Discipleship, Gender Roles, Decision Making and Intimacy
   (with A.B. Spencer, S.R. Tracy and C.G. Tracy)

Joy through the Night: Biblical Resources on Suffering (with A.B. Spencer)

The Prayer Life of Jesus: Shout of Agony, Revelation of Love
   (with A.B. Spencer)

Global Voices in Biblical Equality: Women and Men Serving Together
   in the Church (ed. with A.B. Spencer and M. Haddad)

Reaching for the New Jerusalem: A Biblical and Theological Framework
   for the City (ed. with S.H. Park and A.B. Spencer)

The Global God: Multicultural Evangelical Views of God
   (ed. with A.B. Spencer)

The Goddess Revival: A Christian Response (with A.B. Spencer,
   D.G.F. Hailson and C. Kroeger)

Chanting Down Babylon: The Rastafari Reader (ed. with N.S. Murrell
   and A.A. McFarlane)

2 Corinthians: A Commentary (with A.B. Spencer)

This book is dedicated to Berkeley Street Theatre. My thanks to the Berkeley Street Theatre performers I had the privilege to work with: Gene Burkett, Clancy Dunigan, Charlie Lehman, Gisele Perez, Carol Rowley, Bill Shepherd, and Peggy Vanek-Titus. Special thanks to Peggy Vanek-Titus, the tousle-haired Rubenesque Berkeley Street Theatre actress whose performances rocked Cal campuses in the 1970s. She consulted on this project in so many special ways. Peggy found pictures to include. She reminded me to contact Berkeley Street Theatre members I had forgotten. Her recall of Berkeley Street Theatre memorabilia kicked in when I had memory lapses. Low key and self-effacing, she responded to my calls and consulted tirelessly.

—Jeanne DeFazio

Contents

Acknowledgments

A lot of hard work went into making this book. It was inspired by the creative genius of Drs. William David and Aída Besançon Spencer of *the* House of Prisca and Aquila Series that is published by Wipf and Stock. Thank you to Dr. William David Spencer for reading the manuscript and making helpful suggestions. The text was brilliantly polished and perfected by Mary Riso. This book exists because of those who added their stories to mine (in alphabetical order): Susan Dockery Andrews, Father James Bernstein, Gene Burkett, Charlie Lehman, JMD Myers, Sheri Pedigo, Joanne Petronella, Jozy Pollock, and Olga Soler. Special thanks to Caleb Loring III for his support of this project.

Thanks to the extraordinary Jan Lettieri and Academy Award winning Aaron Mann for consulting on this project and to Matthew W. Martens whose editorial skills helped tremendously. Lynn Jacobs Massetti over the years has given great advice. I am grateful to my wonderful godmother and aunt Fransiska Cano and my aunt Elisa Fernandez for their prayers. My aunt Jane Estremera and her children Rosa, Mark, and Elisa will always be close to my heart for their loving devotion to my mother, Inez DeFazio. Thanks to my aunt Louise Arnerich and my cousin Dan Arnerich for their positive influence on my life. I am grateful for my nieces and nephews Andrew, Bobby, Dino, Dylan, Ella, Francesca, Gian-Carlo, Jeffrey, Jimmy, Karina, Katie, Kogi, Kristen, Lindsey, Merren, Michael, Tommy, and Zach who are all bright lights who make a difference.

My hat is off to Charlie Rose and Anderson Cooper for maintaining high standards in the world of broadcast journalism. Special thanks to Tom Hanks for his extraordinary and inspiring body of work as a film actor. Kudos to Robert Downey Jr. for a remarkable comeback in his acting career. Thanks to Gateway Presbyterian Church of Boston's Reverend Dr. Lawrence PK Mbagara and his wife Anastasia, members Harriet Muthoni Gichuki MacDougal, Douglas MacDougal, Virginia Macharia, Betty Ndungu, Jane Mburu, and Mary Kimani, for their graciousness.

I am grateful to Douglas MacDougal for the extraordinary outreach at the Pilgrim Church in Beverly, MA and the Gateway Presbyterian Church of Boston to the North Shore community. I am indebted to Esther Ngotho, MA in Emergency and Disaster Management and doctoral candidate specializing in Health Advocacy and Leadership, who has been an angel of mercy to me as an affirmative action outreach officer.

Dr. Donald Hilty and my dear friend Dr. Indira Palmatier have encouraged me greatly. Pope Francis's holiness, humor, humility, and practical theology are a powerful witness to Jesus's redemptive love and mercy in this millennial era. Most of all I have Jesus to thank for his heart to serve that made this work possible.

—Jeanne DeFazio

Foreword

David Gill

From 1969 to 1975 the "Christian World Liberation Front"—known everywhere simply as "CWLF"—in Berkeley, California, was one of the liveliest, boldest, and most creative movements on the planet. The Berkeley Street Theatre was one of CWLF's best and brightest expressions and this volume of reminiscence and reflection by actress and editor Jeanne DeFazio is a welcome contribution not just to history but to anyone interested in theatre, theology, evangelism, and culture.

The Christian World Liberation Front was initially a project sponsored by Campus Crusade for Christ (now known as Cru). Founder Jack Sparks (1929 – 2010) grew up on a farm in Indiana and became professor of statistics and research design at Penn State University. At Penn State he got involved with Campus Crusade and decided to leave his academic post and work in campus ministry. While in Santa Barbara during a student uprising which burned a bank to the ground, Jack decided, with Campus Crusade's support, to come to Berkeley, the epicenter of the student movement of the nineteen-sixties and seventies. Within six months or so after its launch CWLF reorganized as an independent, nonprofit, nondenominational outreach to the campus and the counterculture.

CWLF was only in a very secondary sense a reaction to the moribund world of white American Evangelical orthodoxy. Its primary motivation was positive: to share the love of Jesus and the countercultural, life-giving, biblical Gospel in all of its dimensions with a culture in ferment and chaos. Beginning with the Free Speech Movement in the fall of 1964 (my freshman year at the University of California, Berkeley), the universities of the world, not just in the United States, exploded in protests and demonstrations. Radical political movements against colonialism around the world often called themselves "Liberation Fronts." Adopting this language, the "Third World Liberation Front" was a movement at Berkeley during my junior and senior years demanding the inclusion of ethnic studies and a broader education than the Eurocentric focus of the time.

Barely two years later, the Christian World Liberation Front was launched in Berkeley. Jack and Esther Sparks, with their four young children, rented a house near the Cal campus in early 1969 during the Peoples' Park controversy. That controversy had thousands demonstrating in Berkeley streets against the university's attempt to evict a street people/hippie encampment on one of its empty lots to begin a building project (Note: it is still a "peoples' park" five decades later!). The demonstrations resulted in one shooting death by police. Demonstrations, sit-ins, marches, protests, and police responses were a constant beginning in 1964. I have often joked that I have a hard time studying unless I can smell tear gas because the two are so closely associated in my experience!

It wasn't just about students and university policies. It was the Vietnam War and the military draft. It was the Black Panthers in neighboring Oakland, civil rights, Martin Luther King, Jr., and Malcolm X. It was the early feminist movement and the environmental movement. And more broadly it was the hippies and the counterculture looking for freedom, community, and meaning, often accompanied by a cloud of marijuana smoke. My other sixties joke is that former President Bill Clinton said that he smoked marijuana just once but didn't inhale; whereas I, the same age, *never* smoked a joint but I "inhaled all the time" (referring to the clouds of such smoke one walked past regularly!). Sexual chaos, conflict between the generations, and disruption of all the old ways—this was the context into which the CWLF founders plunged.

From his Campus Crusade for Christ background, Jack Sparks brought a passionate faith in Jesus Christ and a bold, militant commitment to be present and bear witness absolutely anywhere possible. When Jack came to Berkeley, he left behind him the conservative, traditional formulas and allegiances of Campus Crusade and the American Evangelical establishments in order to be fully, radically, and simply present in the culture as a disciple of Jesus. He took St. Paul quite literally about "becoming all things to all people in order to win them." Bearded and bib-overalled, Jack blended into the campus and counterculture very quickly and only emerged six years later (to the astonishment of all of us who worked with him during those CWLF years) to become part of an Orthodox Church leadership team in a very different calling and setting.

The Christian World Liberation Front shared some commonalities with the "Jesus People" movements around the world at the time and was often included in news articles and books on that topic. Staff leaders like Bill Squires, Arnie Bernstein, Howard "Lono" Criss, and Ken "Koala Bear" Winkle oversaw several urban residence houses and the rural "Rising Son Ranch," which provided housing and caring relationships. Hundreds of hippies, "flower children," dope users, and countercultural drop-outs found acceptance, care, redemption, and new life through the loving outreach of Jack and his CWLF "Forever Family" colleagues. The Monday Night Bible studies were open, honest, free, and exhilarating; the music growing out of the experience was catchy, singable, inspiring, and often amazingly deep.

CWLF also meant rallies on Sproul Steps at Cal; baptisms in Strawberry Creek; Christian alternative rock concerts; food giveaways, picketing, and protesting against war and for the gospel in Golden Gate or Flamingo Park, against the exploitation of women and for the gospel in North Beach—rattling the cages of wannabe religious gurus and frauds, complacent liberal Protestants, and fearful, backward-looking fundamentalists and evangelicals.

CWLF was also politically and socially thoughtful and engaged. CWLF leaders shared much in common with the early Sojourners movement in Chicago and then Washington DC and with the Anabaptist/Mennonite approach of John Howard Yoder and others. CWLF's concerns about poverty, homelessness, sexism, racism, warfare (Vietnam was usually the focus), and violence were genuine and often led to concrete actions and participation in larger debates, demonstrations, and even the political party conventions of 1972. Some of this participation was witness *with* others concerned about the issues, but it was also witness *to* other movements about a deeper perspective rooted in Jesus Christ. Walt and Ginny Hearn inspired many to pursue "simple living" less wedded to a culture of consumption, conflict, and indulgence.

CWLF was especially distinctive from both the Jesus Movement and the Evangelical Political Activists in its educational orientation. Jack had been a public university professor and was intensely committed to interaction with Berkeley as a university community and to the combat of ideas—not just the saving of individual souls for the afterlife. Jack's passion for learning attracted many other Christians influenced by Francis Schaeffer's L'Abri movement and Regent College's new presence at the University of British Columbia. The Spiritual Counterfeits Project led by Brooks Alexander and others pursued a serious study and exposé of the fraudulent cults and gurus on the scene at the time. "The Crucible: A Forum for Radical Christian Studies" was launched by David Gill, Bernie Adeney, and their colleagues as a sort of "L'Abri" study group and counterpart to the various "free universities" cropping up as alternatives to Cal Berkeley. [The Crucible was folded into the New College Berkeley graduate school in 1978]. In 1971 Sharon Gallagher and David Gill began co-editing CWLF's tabloid "Right On," which Jack had launched in 1969 as an alternative to the "Berkeley Barb." Although CWLF ended in the mid-1970s, Gallagher has continued its publication legacy as editor from 1973 to the present of *Radix Magazine* with copy editor Ginny Hearn and a long list of writers, art directors, and illustrators like Keith Criss and Larry Hatfield, photographer Steve Sparks, and other contributors.

It is impossible to list all the individuals and ministries that directly or indirectly owe much of their inspiration to Jack Sparks and the CWLF he founded. Moishe Rosen got some of his inspiration for starting "Jews for Jesus" from CWLF. All across North America non-Christians were intrigued by what was happening—wanting to know more about Jesus as a result. And churches of all kinds were inspired to rethink their own discipleship and outreach in more creative and radical biblical terms.

So it was in this context that CWLF's Street Theatre initiative arose—the initiative about which you will read in this book. I remember vividly a talk Jack Sparks gave on "Creative Evangelism" in which he reminded us of a long list of creative theatrical initiatives by the prophets. Here are just a few examples of God designing some prophetic street theatre:

- Jeremiah buys a new loincloth and after wearing it awhile hides it in the cleft of a rock near the river; some time later he retrieves it and uses the ruined loincloth to represent the rot in a disobedient, unfaithful people (Jer 13).

- Jeremiah buys an earthen jug, and after reproving the elders of the people throws it to the ground and smashes it to represent the coming disaster owing to their misbehavior (Jer 19)

- Jeremiah makes a "yoke of straps" and puts it around his neck to represent the oppression about to be endured—and then has another prophet come and take it off of his neck to represent God's promise of deliverance (Jer 27-28).

- Seraiah is told to read aloud from a scroll detailing the disasters coming on Babylon and when he is finished to tie a rock around it and heave it into the Euphrates River while the people watch in shock, to show "thus shall Babylon sink and rise no more" (Jer 51).

- Ezekiel is told to build a little model city on a brick and set it up (in full view of city leaders) with toy siege works, walls, ramps, and battering rams—then to lie next to it on his left side for some days, then turn and lie on his right side . . . And this is just the beginning of Ezekiel's prophetic theatre! (Ezek 4).

Little wonder that the imaginations of our CWLF Street Theatre group directors and actors were unleashed! So on Berkeley's central Sproul Plaza you might have heard someone like me give a public CWLF talk on how true peace requires a spiritual foundation in knowing Jesus Christ, not just in ending a horrible war. But you just as likely might have seen a troupe of six or ten of our Street Theatre actors drawing a crowd to their prophetic performance. We loved these brothers and sisters and their witness. Conversations with bystanders and students passing through on the way to class followed these performances.

By 1975 times had changed and the CWLF changed as well, dropping the "Liberation Front" name that now felt like a pretentious cliché. But many of CWLF's ministries continued under other names and other auspices. And the people, who were at the heart of these initiatives, including our actors, playwrights, and directors, carried their gifts, talents, and experiences off with them to bless and inspire countless others.

> *David Gill went on after CWLF to do a PhD at the University of Southern California and to become a seminary and business school professor for forty years and a widely published author.*

Introduction

Jeanne DeFazio

Left to right, Keith Criss, Lono Criss, Clancy Dunigan, Charlie Lehman,
Peggy Vanek-Titus, and Carol Rowley in "Registration"

This book is written by street performers. It reflects on the impact of street theater in our contemporary world and consists of autobiographical accounts of Christian performing artists who put sneakers on the Gospel and took it to the streets. The book identifies street theater as an exciting and creative way to shine Jesus's light. It describes how artists across the globe outreached in street performances uniquely suited to each culture. It demonstrates how and why street performers have great intimacy with the audience and the opportunity to transform lives through redemptive drama. It offers testimonies from world class performing artists telling their own stories of what brought them to receive Jesus and how the power of his death and resurrection on the cross helped them through the challenges in their lives.

My vision was to edit a book with each performer modeling through testimony effective ways to outreach on the street. This book is the fulfillment of that vision. William David Spencer suggested I set up each chapter with a brief introduction I wrote followed by the first person account of each of these powerful ministers of Jesus's redemptive love. Chronicling forty-five years of worldwide outreach, this work has unique historic value. It introduces the reader to Christians who engaged in highly creative and innovative ways to outreach. The book features original contributions from (in alphabetical order) Susan Dockery Andrews, Father James Bernstein, Gene Burkett, Jeanne DeFazio, Charlie Lehman, JMD Myers, Sheri Pedigo, Joanne Petronella, Jozy Pollock, and Olga Soler. These are evangelists who love Jesus and shared their faith through their art. Chapter by chapter, each author models how to foster teamwork and perform skillfully with a flexible, upbeat, and fun attitude. Each author describes the spiritual benefit of sharing God's word, praying, and spending fun time together. Each chapter concludes with an invitation to Christians gifted in the performing arts to shed God's light by performing in the street.

Through the ministries of these compelling and talented artists, Jesus called the culture of the time to the wedding feast of the Lamb,[1] the culmination of human history when God and his beloved church are joined forever. I have seen the love and sensitivity of these artists to the Holy Spirit who enabled each to bring Jesus's message through each one's chosen medium. It has been one of my greatest blessings to work professionally with the contributors to this book. I know that they will be a blessing to you as you meet them here for the first time, or deepen your relationship with them if you have already enjoyed their work.

---

1. Rev 19:6-9: "Then I heard what seemed to be the voice of a great multitude, like the sound of many waters and like the sound of mighty thunder peals, crying out, 'Hallelujah! For the Lord our God the Almighty reigns. Let us rejoice and exult and give him the glory, for the marriage of the Lamb has come, and his bride has made herself ready; to her it has been granted to be clothed with fine linen, bright and pure'—for the fine linen is the righteous deeds of the saints. And the angel said to me, 'Write this: Blessed are those who are invited to the marriage supper of the Lamb.' And he said to me, 'These are true words of God'" (NRSV).

PART 1

Christian Guerilla Theater Then

Berkeley Street Theatre

*The Jesus Revolution and the California Dream Merge
in a Dramatic Outpouring of the Holy Spirit*

Jeanne DeFazio

Jeanne DeFazio performing in *Choose or Lose* on Sproul Plaza,
at the UC Berkeley Campus, 1974

In the mid-1970s, many ideologies and cultures merged on Sproul Plaza, the gateway to the UC Berkeley Campus. Clancy Dunigan describes Berkeley Street Theatre's integral part of that cultural mix:

> The 1970s, the Berkeley Campus was a cauldron of activism, and lunch table politics of the right, left, and center. Berkeley Street Theatre was part of the mix, along with religious outlaws, former university professors, Marxists, gay and straight activists, Jews for Jesus, Anabaptists, Southern Folk, Bronx Puerto Ricans, New York Theater Actors, Floridians seminary trained, marrieds, ex-addicts, and all true believers around the USA. Berkeley-bound, they took buses, planes, cars, or bummed rides looking for the kindness of strangers spiced with God's grace and street savvy lessons. There were PhDs, BAs, no degrees, and a few Bible college professors. Mars Hill could have been next door, but instead it was the Berkeley Free Kitchen, where Steve Jobs also bummed and ate. Get the picture?[1]

The California Dream

In the dedication of the book entitled *Creative Ways to Build Christian Community*, I reflect on the impact of this California awakening on my spiritual journey: "This book is dedicated to all those who feel God tugging at their heartstrings to serve him. If you are feeling unworthy to serve God, you are not alone. My youth was spent in the time and state of 'California Dreamin.'"[2] The 1970s' mass migration to the UC Berkeley campus was a direct result of the unique phenomenon known as the California Dream, which historically identified the desire to "get rich quick" during the California Gold Rush Days (1849). By the administration of Governor Edmund G. Brown Jr., it manifested as a tuition-free, world-class University of California education. I attended UC Berkeley in 1971 and in 1974 graduated from the University of California at Davis. After graduation, I visited the Berkeley campus, and saw a production of Berkeley Street Theatre on Sproul Plaza. I was struck by the authenticity of the performance and shocked that there was a Christian message. After the performance, I spoke with the actors and asked if I could join the group. Just previous to joining,

1. Clancy Dunigan, Street Theatre member, interview by email, December 2010.

2. "California Dreamin'" is a song written by John Phillips and Michelle Phillips in 1963, and made famous by The Mamas and the Papas.

I met Jack Sparks, founder of the high profile Christian World Liberation Front, on Telegraph Avenue. He smiled at me and sensed the burden in my heart. I looked at all the people in the street and said, *I don't know how to help these people.* If you had seen Telegraph Avenue in the 1970s, you would understand. It was the boulevard of the broken California Dream for so many runaways and lost souls. I recall the sad looking young people strung out on drugs, lying on the street, while Krishna devotees, wearing orange togas, chanting and drumming with shaved heads, passed among them. So many displaced young people looking for the California Dream found their way to the Telegraph Avenue street scene. Many needy and lost people lived a nightmare on the streets. Jack understood my concern and assured me that God would use me to reach the heartbroken for Jesus as an actress in Berkeley Street Theatre. With Jack's encouragement, in 1974, I joined Berkeley Street Theatre, eager to use my passion for theater to reach the disenchanted and despairing with the message of Jesus's redemptive love.

Asked in the troupe's newsletter to share my thoughts and feelings as a Christian doing street theater for the first time, I concluded: *When I recall the huge responsive audiences, all the wonderful people I have met, and the honor that it has been to serve God with my work, I am most happy.*[3]

Looking back, it is clear that my journey to Berkeley Street Theatre was providential. Reared in a large Italian/Spanish Roman Catholic family, I felt the love and presence of Jesus when I was a child attending Roman Catholic schools and the Catholic Church. As a junior at the University of California, I said the "sinner's prayer" with a "born again" friend, expecting nothing at all like what happened. As C.S. Lewis described in his autobiographical work, *Surprised by Joy*,[4] I felt Jesus's presence and great joy, and began attending both Catholic charismatic as well as Protestant evangelical services.[5]

Through all the twists and turns of my spiritual journey, the Holy Spirit impressed upon me the words of Exodus 23:20: "I am going to send an angel in front of you, to guard you on the way and to bring you to the place that I have prepared" (NRSV). I realize now that these performing artists were "angels"[6] who God sent to guide me. Each day as I joined with

---

3. *Berkeley Street Theatre Newsletter*, Spring 1975.

4. Lewis, *Surprised by Joy*, vii.

5. DeFazio and Spencer, *Redeeming the Screens*, xiv–xv. "Used by permission of Wipf and Stock Publishers." www.wipfandstock.com.

6. *Malak*, a messenger specifically of God, short definition: angel. The word occurs

this group to rehearse under the direction of Gene Burkett, I learned the craft of street theater. In Berkeley Street Theatre I had the opportunity to pray and to grow spiritually in a community of unusually forward-minded and caring performers who put their hearts and souls into making their own Christian experience real to audiences.

One Whole Earth Day in the spring of 1975, Berkeley Street Theatre performed on the University of California Davis campus. My parents attended the performance and had mixed feelings. They invited the Berkeley Street Theatre members to lunch after the performance. In conversation afterward, my father complimented my friends from Berkeley Street Theatre. He did not understand the drive to create alternative theater, but he discerned in that group genuinely positive young people who were living out their convictions in an innovative and interesting way. I had supported myself as a waitress in local Berkeley restaurants and coffee houses while participating in Berkeley Street Theatre. After seeing the performance, my dad supported my experience by paying down my student loans each month. That was a big thing for him to do at the time.

Berkeley Street Theatre's Dramatic Outpouring of the Holy Spirit

In 2010, I met with former Berkeley Street Theatre members in a coffee house on Shattuck Avenue in Berkeley, California. Over three decades later, we paused to reflect on Berkeley Street Theatre and the lasting impact of the Jesus Movement: the contemporary Christian music and literature explosion in the 1960s and 1970s, which led to widespread Christian TV, radio, and other media entertainment after the 1970s. While we chatted, very polished and polite young Asian tourists at an adjacent table took our photos and asked me questions about us. I explained that Berkeley Street Theatre was a talented and prayerful team that successfully brought youth to Jesus. How? Revelation 12:11 explains it: "We were victorious by the blood of the Lamb and the word of his testimony" (Aramaic Bible in Plain English). I want to conclude by encouraging readers to use their performing talents in Christian outreach on the streets. If I can help you in anyway contact me: jcdefazio55@gmail.com.

---

213 times in the Old Testament, *James Strong's Exhaustive Concordance* #4397, www. bibletools.com.

Resources

View LeaAnn Pendergrass's Uniting the Nations interview with Jeanne De-Fazio: https://www.youtube.com/watch?v=nSFMoAJuPRk. View LeaAnn Pendergrass interview of Gemma Wenger: http://www.thecrosstv.com/media-gallery/918-uniting-the-nations-6-16-15?category_id=237.

2

Choose or Lose

Gene Burkett

Left to right: Gene Burkett, Peggy Vanek-Titus, Jeanne DeFazio, Clancy Dunigan, Bill
Shepherd, Charlie Lehman, Susan Dockery, and Carol Rowley in *The Museum*

Eugene H. Burkett (Gene) was a member of Christian World Liberation Front from 1972 to 1975, director of the Berkeley Street Theatre, and member of the CWLF Leaders Council. He graduated from South Dade High School in Homestead, Florida in 1966. In 1970, he received a BA in Speech from the University of South Florida in Tampa and went on to complete an MA in Speech from the University of South Florida in 1972. He received a California Community College Teaching Credential and a California Adult School Teaching Credential in 1976, and became an agent for John Hancock Life Insurance Company in Oakland, CA in 1977. In 1978, Gene qualified for a California Life and Health Insurance License. Gene has worked for Insurance Link in Capitola, CA since 1991, becoming the owner and president in 2008. He also received CASA (Court Appointed Special Advocate) training and certification in Santa Cruz, CA in 1996. In 2008, Gene became a Life in Learning Institute (LILI) graduate in insurance leadership training, which is part of the National Association of Financial Advisors. He completed Dominican Hospital Auxiliary Training and Certification in Santa Cruz, CA in 2009. From 2009 to 2011, Gene's further educational experience included church leaders' training and vision planning, various vocal choir singing, chanting and choir directors' workshops and seminars, and dozens of continuing education classes to maintain a California insurance license.

Gene is married to Peggy (Anna) Burkett and they have four children: David, Justin, Erik, and Catherine. Gene and Anna have three grandchildren and have lived in Felton, CA since 1984. Gene is a member of St. Lawrence Orthodox Church in Felton where he sings in the choir, is a cantor, and is the director of the social committee. He is a member of the National Association of Insurance and Financial Advisors (NAIFA). He is a past president of his local association and is currently its National Committeeman.

I recently contacted Gene Burkett for the first time in thirty years. He responded immediately. It was almost as if I was that twenty-five-year old amateur actress again. Each time I asked Gene for artistic advice on this project he responded with amazing guidance. Gene is low key and brilliant. He does not advertise his talent; instead, he gets you to be the best you can be. Here is his story.

I came to Berkeley in the fall of 1972 just after receiving an MA in Speech with an emphasis in Oral Interpretation that summer. I spent the previous four years in college in performance, and directing fiction and non-fiction adapted for the stage. My former college roommate Frank Couch had started a street theater in Berkeley with the Christian World Liberation Front. Frank asked me to come to Berkeley and join him.

I joined CWLF[1] at this time, when I was searching for a meaningful Christianity. I wanted a faith that related to my entire being. I needed something much more than attending church on Sunday and then having an unrelated secular life for the rest of the week. I wasn't really a radical, nor did I really relate to the countercultural scene. To paraphrase David in Psalm 28:7: The Lord strengthened, protected, and guided me in Berkeley Street Theatre; the Lord was my strength and my shield, my heart trusted in him, and I was helped; therefore, my heart greatly rejoices and with my song, I will praise him.

Frank had a speech degree and had worked in oral interpretation with me. Frank was also very involved with the Vietnam protests in the 1960s. He saw the theater in terms of making political statements that emphasized a Christian point of view in current events and in the personal life choices of individuals. He was concerned with the artistic merits of the production and the acting abilities of the performers—but these things were of secondary importance. After I spent a year with the group, Frank decided to return to his roots on the East Coast.

I had been directing and acting for the theater group and so was asked to become the director when Frank left. I took the position of director of the street theater because I was interested in showing the impact of Christianity on people's lives. I felt it was important to show the depth of the Christian experience to non-Christians in a way that was artistic and spoke directly to the people of the counterculture in the early 1970s. Berkeley Street Theatre performed on college campuses, centering mostly on Sproul Plaza at UC Berkeley. I wanted the theater group to have a name that identified it with Berkeley so I renamed CWLF Street Theater the Berkeley Street Theatre. This name was recognizable to people in a much broader way than if it had a name such as the Lord Jesus Players.

The Christian church has a long history of using theater to inspire people in the culture of the day. Long ago, the church in the Holy Land had people follow the last hours of Christ through progressions to spots on the way to the cross, enacting the events at the actual sites. During the Middle Ages in Europe, morality plays were performed in the front of the church

1. The Christian World Liberation Front was the high profile Christian outreach to the counterculture featured in the cover story, "The Jesus Revolution," *Time Magazine*, 21 June 1971.

to educate the populace in the importance of Christianity in their lives. *The Hound of Everyman* is such a play. The church wanted to reach people with the impact of God in the lives of those both in and outside of the church. This was a culture that was saturated with Christianity, even if many stayed outside of the church. The people were well aware of the tenets of the faith, but often lacked something to show them that each person needed Christ and that Christ was inviting them into the church. It was my belief that the students of the 1970s were less influenced by the church than those who lived in the Middle Ages in Europe, but that they still lived in a culture that was shaped by the church.

As director, I worked on coming up with plays; we called them performances, since these were plays that were constantly reworked and sometimes had to be adapted to the audience. At times the crowds consisted of at least five hundred people. We had members of CWLF come and help us attract a crowd by just being there, ready for the play to begin.

The plays I came up with at first were related to issues common to college students. One show was called *Choose or Lose* and was based on a young man's life from birth to death, with each part of his life enacted as part of a game show that was well known to TV audiences of the 1950s and 1960s. In the end our hero, Willy Nilly, had the opportunity of choosing one of three doors and he chose door number three. That door opened to death. We killed him with a large plastic hammer and carried him away. This play had the intent of showing that life, unless there is a choice made for something like Christianity, will lead to death. I call this a pre-Christian message.

Charlie Lehman and Susan Dockery, two street theater members, also wrote shows. Charlie's was called *Registration* and was done entirely with us acting out government forms. In *Registration*, government forms represented the extent of the bureaucratic control over individual lives, particularly the students enrolling in state university campuses. At the end of the play we handed out a flyer that related to the play and linked it to the message. Susan's production was an adaptation of C.S. Lewis's *The Great Divorce*. In the show, residents of hell are taken to heaven and given a chance to repent and choose heaven. Some choose heaven and some choose to remain in hell.

I came up with several other plays. One was called *Collage* and was a string of TV and print ad commercials that showed the shallowness of life. The Christ figure wore white face and kept appearing throughout the show. In the last scene, the Christ figure held hands with all the actors and they moved in a circle. One of the players broke the circle and the actors were left gasping on the ground unable to breathe. Christ came to each one and offered to breathe into their mouths. Some of the players accepted the breath and rejoined the circle, while others refused and slowly died on the ground. After one performance an audience member cried out, "My group has 50 percent more salvations than your group." To those from the 1960s that was a play on a Crest toothpaste commercial, which told consumers that they could expect fewer cavities than if they used other leading brands. It told me the audience got the message.

My favorite production was *The Prodigal Son*. I imagined that there were many prodigals on the streets and on the campus of Berkeley. I switched the perspective of the parable and placed the city where the prodigal goes after leaving his father in the foreground. All the scenes after the son leaves his father are played out as different "trips" in Berkeley—such as a street singer singing to a group who decided to pair off while listening to the music. After each scene one of the players strips the son of an article of clothing. The son is left in the end only wearing pants. At this point the players surround him, stroking him and chanting, "I am you and you are me." This scene, in which the prodigal son is demoralized by the way he is being treated in the world, finally causes him to run home to his father. The son comes to his senses and sees his father in the distance and returns to him. When he returns to the father, the son kneels before the father who places a red velvet robe around him. I was able to be in the audience because this was one show in which I did not participate as an actor. Being in the audience, I heard people say, "This is the Prodigal Son." This is exactly what I hoped for; we reached them artistically and emotionally, and then they put the pieces together themselves. I wanted our presentation to be just as good as any secular performance. I did not want to preach to them about Jesus and then hear them say, "Oh another rap about Jesus."

Some people were angered by the performances when they were confronted by Jesus in the context of something familiar to them, and they did not like that. However, we received exceptionally nice reactions too. Both Christians and non-Christians came up to talk to us after the show. People accepted Jesus as Savior after Berkeley Street Theatre performances. The average audience member watched our performances, enjoyed it as it exposed a serious Christian message, and left. Our crowds usually ran from two hundred to three hundred, and many of the audience members watched the shows several times over the years.

We performed mostly in Berkeley on Sproul Plaza. We also performed at Stanford, San Francisco State, Sonoma State, Cal Poly in San Luis Obispo, De Anza College, Washington State in Seattle, and the University of Northern Arizona in Flagstaff. It was a heady experience and it was a time when students were ready to stop and give their attention to a twenty to twenty-five-minute performance. I was privileged to work with a dedicated team of actors over those years. Some had acting experience and some had never acted before. We became a very cohesive group who spent a good deal of time together improving our skills and perfecting our shows.

I would like to express my gratitude to Berkeley Street Theatre artists and dedicated Christians for this life-changing time in my life. Please do contact me at the address below if you are interested in forming a Christian theater group and have any questions, or need advice or support.

Resources

Gene Burkett's email address: Gene@insurancelink.biz

3

Registration

Charlie Lehman

Left to right Arnie Bernstein and Charlie Lehman in *Registration*

Charlie Lehman graduated from Queens College, City University of New York, in 1972 with a BA in theater. He received a paralegal certificate from the University of California, Los Angeles Extension, in 1983 and a certificate in private investigation from Cal State Fullerton Extension in 2006. In 2016 he retired from the Los Angeles County Public Defender's office after twenty-five years as a paralegal.

Charlie was an actor who loved the craft. I recall that every move that Charlie made as an actor seemed right. I recall his ability to cover for any lost line or cue in a live performance. I often walked off stage and thanked him for his professional generosity. Recently, I spoke with him for the first time in over thirty years. I was struck by the effortless way Charlie continues to respond as a key player in the drama of life. While consulting Charlie on this project I found him habitually picking up my literary lost lines and cues. He mailed me relevant notes to include in the text, sent me pictures and a book for reference, and has connected me to many Berkeley Street Theatre members. He also has encouraged me. The way in which he continued to cover for me professionally has really touched my heart. As he himself explains:

We are taught about the world and ourselves in theaters. Today there isn't much recognition of the risen Christ there, and that omission or mockery teaches the audience. Having been shaped by drama for good or for ill all of my life, I want Christians to be involved in the production of quality drama.

During my years in Berkeley, I did not see our work as that of evangelists. We were actors. Our plays were evangelistic but they were more like the parables of Jesus (Storytelling is an art, too.) and the actions of the prophets than like the work of first century evangelists, twentieth century evangelists, or those in between.

I would be nothing without God. Without a Creator I would not exist. Without a Redeemer I would be guilty and scared and miserable. The lordship of Christ has given my life the right direction. As a theater student in my last year at Queens College, I wanted to do Christian theater but there was nothing on the horizon: no groups I could join, and no vocations. I prayed about this during my senior year. God gave me a vocation out of nowhere. Less than two months after graduating, I was doing Christian street theater in Berkeley as a member of Berkeley Street Theatre. I thank God for that.

Father Jack Sparks, founder of Christian World Liberation Front, did not come off like the ex-statistics professor that he was. He was a poetic Christian community organizer with a big heart. He welcomed people like the members of our street theater group and let us loose. In street theater, I had all the artistic freedom I could handle; it was a good thing all the other people were there to contribute and to lead. We worked up our plays, mostly satire from a Christian perspective, in rehearsal. We cut loose on Sproul Plaza in Berkeley, at San Francisco State, and at other campuses and venues as well as on tours in the Southwest and the Northwestern states.

In the summer of 1975, Jeanne DeFazio and I went out on a limb. With the blessing of Berkeley Street Theatre director Gene Burkett, we traveled to New York City, recruited, trained, and rehearsed with actors found through the InterVarsity Christian Fellowship, and performed one of our plays in a tiny park near the 1976 Democratic National Convention and several City University campuses. We pulled it off, thank God; the New York audiences were as warm as those in Berkeley.

Registration

Berkeley Street Theatre's *Registration* contrasted the interests of bureaucracies in all of us and God's loving interest in each of us. If you filled out an application to enroll in a UC campus you would see why this was true. The nature of the personal questions that were to be answered and the way that personal information was depersonalized in bureaucratic application forms was stressed in this play. Berkeley Street Theatre worked up this play collectively. An incident, idea, story, painting or, in this case, government forms, inspired the director. The director has something to say to the audience. (Example: one of *Registration's* characters delivers an exhortation from the prophet Hosea 4:1: "There is no faithfulness, or kindness or knowledge of God in the land" (NASB), and the director used *Registration's* satire of the tyranny of government forms to say it strongly and artistically through the actions of the characters.)

How Berkeley Street Theatre merged improvisation and street theater as a Christian outreach to the counterculture

Berkeley Street Theatre Street's Summer 1975 internship program put together a play out of six short plays. The first week of the internship was run like a five-day workshop. On the second part of each day the interns worked on the plays. There were three groups and each group had four interns and was directed by a Berkeley Street Theatre staff actor. In this program the director was not always the one who had the idea for the play. The play I directed came from an idea one of the interns got from a painting. The short plays I saw on the fifth day were good and united in their message. Here is where I saw the Lord's coordination: each group did not know what the other groups were doing or that I wanted to make a full length play from three short pieces. In each of these three short plays, characters had to choose God or turn from Him. So I reshuffled the groups and told them to come up with three scenes that had to fit with three short plays already performed to make up one long play. The interns created three good pieces of guerilla theater.

Guerrilla Theater

The word guerrilla refers to a band carrying on irregular warfare. This word has come to identify a genre of theater. Guerrilla theater is a striking form of theater, usually performed without sets, and out of doors. Street theater is a synonym. The guerrilla actor, like the guerrilla soldier, does not have the technical aids that many in his profession expect. Adaptability, mobility, financial and therefore ideological freedom from the audience, and an extraordinary involvement in the creation of the play are some advantages of guerrilla theater over legitimate theater.

Street theater is not bountifully equipped or recognized. Most obviously there is no theater building or all that that implies—lights, a stage, and seats for which your audience has paid. Guerrilla actors compensate. They find an area with lots of people, and a place where a loud performance would be tolerated and attended. They arrive at least one hour before the time of the performance. They have plenty to do. They announce the show in loud, short phrases: i.e., "Free performance here at noon!" and on portable cardboard signs (three-foot by two-foot signs are helpful). The guerrilla theater team invites passersby to the show and briefly answers their questions. The actors put on their makeup at the site of the performance.

The play itself will be visually and aurally striking from the start. All the actors or one or two may be in a "freeze" position. Or they may start off the show in slow motion. The show may begin in total silence. Or all the performers may be talking loudly at once (the huzzah technique) to be suddenly silenced by a prearranged cue. All these techniques are powerfully used for contrast and varied to fit the needs of the show and the situation. They can be used throughout the show, one after another, when they are appropriate. For example, there are no sets and frozen actors take the place of these sets (rooms, forests, caves, etc).

Discipline is essential. Holding a freeze for several minutes is hard work. Good slow motion is very hard. The concentration of the actors and the attendant precision and strength of their movements and sound make a performance strong. If the cast is frozen and one actor scratches his chin on his shoulder, this mistake will be the focus of the audience. If a frozen actor just moves his upper lip, perhaps ten people will notice. He has failed those ten people. The same is true for slow motion: faces, fingers, and feet must all move slowly. Because guerrilla theater performances are short, a large part of the meaning is communicated visually, and long speeches are not used. Every word must be understood by the audience; every word must be loud and clear (unless it is meant to be unintelligible to the audience). If only one word is soft or garbled, many in the audience will miss much that they were meant to hear. If all these lapses are exceptions, they detract from a performance; if they are the rule, they make up a poor, uniformly sloppy show. Practice and concentration make the difference.

The play is written or rewritten to suit the purposes of the guerrilla team. Because most of the audience has not planned to attend the play until they see the actors, minutes before it began or come in minutes before or later, they cannot be expected to watch an hour of theater. They had not planned it so most of them don't have the time. The play should be about ten to forty minutes long; the team should make the point quickly and strongly, before the audience has to leave. The beginning, as I mentioned before, should attract attention. It should fit the rest of the show, but it should not contain material essential to the understanding of the play, because not all audience members will see the very beginning. The content of the play is in the action, complemented by an economical use of understandable, important words. The theater group writes (often there is no script) the play in rehearsal; when a script or another piece of art, like a poem or a painting is used, it is drastically altered by the group to fill the needs of guerrilla theater. Although the guerrilla theater actor is not compensated or recognized to the extent that the Broadway actor or the Hollywood actor is, he has some advantages over both of them. Because he needs no stage and little equipment (makeup, costumes, a couple of signs, and a couple of props), he has great mobility and financial independence. He is not required to pander to the audience; he can upset them if he feels they need to be upset. A disciplined group can cheaply and easily present their ideas publicly, without dependence upon the "media." For some groups like those participating in the anti-war movement and most Christian groups, among others, street theater is often the only kind of theater within reach. Sometimes guerrilla theater is the only way to reach the audience—for example, on a college campus— that you want to reach.

Guerrilla theater takes on added meaning for the Christian. It is not only the genre of theater previously described. It is not only ideological struggle. For example, there was a lot of street theater at the time that reflected the ideological struggles of the anti-Vietnam war movement. This might be distinguished from the alternative street theater that was a common sight on Sproul plaza and that was both cultural and political. A performance of Christian guerrilla theater is using spiritual warfare as described by Paul the apostle in Ephesians 6: 19: "And for me, that utterance may be given unto me, that I may open my mouth boldly, to make known the mystery of the gospel" (NIV). Berkeley Street Theatre actors opened their mouths boldly to make known the mystery of the gospel. As the Holy Spirit spoke to the audience, the forces of Satan tempted and assaulted the actors. The actors prayed for themselves and the audiences. All kinds of disconcerting things happened before and after the performances. Actors arrived late and people harassed the actors. Actors needed to trust God to use the performances to speak to God's audience: the people He created and whom He loves. The best Christian performers, doing an excellent job, cannot change a person's heart—only God can.

Who were the members of Berkeley Street Theatre?

The most important thing about Berkeley Street Theatre members was their commitment to Christ and their desire to do good Christian theater. The group was made up of middle-class college students and college dropouts in their early twenties. Some came from all over the country and from various churches as well as ungodly backgrounds.

We did not start out as guerilla theater specialists. Many of us majored in disciplines that were important to the guerilla actor: oral interpretation, theater, and dance. Many of us had no previous training. We were not fully prepared for what we did. We brought our talents and our weaknesses to the group. I came to Berkeley with a weak voice. Back at Queens College when I would do a scene well, my acting teacher would say, "That's good Charlie, except for your voice." In our early shows I sometimes ground up my voice so badly, that I could not be heard by the end of the show. We prayed about my voice and I concentrated on it. I had to speak slower, give myself enough breath, open my mouth wider, and consciously relax my throat. I once had the weakest voice in the group. Later, I had the strongest.

Performance

Performances are subjectively discerned by actors and directors. Performance scared me for years. As time went on, it challenged and excited me, and I felt exhilarated after a show. When I watched a show I directed, the mistakes are what stood out. The actors may have knocked themselves out and have been thinking on their feet and I saw the mistakes. We didn't discuss mistakes after a performance. The actors could expect to hear about their mistakes at the next rehearsal.

The Actor

An actor is a person who communicates theatrical reality. Theatrical reality is a fiction that both the audience and the actor believe. Actors believe in what they are doing on stage even though they know they are actors. They share the special happenings of theatrical reality with the audience. The actor's imagination and his concentration on the "game" he is playing ("player" is a synonym for actor) makes it real to him, and the precision and clarity of what he does communicates this reality to the audience. The audience sees the actor dealing with imaginary circumstances and reacting with his body to the other actors and to the imaginary environment. The actor makes it possible for the audience to accept the theatrical reality and get involved in it.

The Audience

Over the years I thought about our audiences. God created them just as He has created me. He loves them more than I could. I trusted that He used our shows as one of many experiences in their lives to call them to Himself. Sometimes an audience was small or unresponsive. Some people watched intently while others did not care about us at all. I reminded myself that as an actor I owed everyone a good show.

What did people who attended the shows see? Over the years we learned a lot about street theater. People did not buy tickets to see Berkeley Street Theatre performances. We arrived on campus and performed. Sometimes the local Christian group had already publicized the performance. We prayed and put on our makeup in public and announced our show, using our voices and large signs, at the site of our performance—which was usually at an open place near the cafeteria or student union. As a street theater group we needed no sets or amplification. Using a few props we usually performed outside, and we never charged our audiences. Our plays were striking and fast moving—about half an hour—so our audiences would not lose interest. We strived to make our plays artistically sound and clear.

A Day in the Life of Berkeley Street Theatre

November 24, 1975. It was a ridiculous day. It had been seriously planned. Meet at 6:30 am, arrive at Irvington High School in Fremont, CA at 8:30 am, and perform in all of one Christian teacher's four drama classes and at lunch time in the plaza. Things started to fall apart at 5:15 am.

Arriving happily on time, I put the plywood Christian street theater sign in my trunk. My trunk lid usually falls like an anvil but that day the latch wasn't working. Slam, Slam, Slam: good morning neighbors. Our director, who was the owner and driver of our Impala, was missing. Great, that means five people in my Camaro, including one on the padded cinderblock on the back seat. Since I was the assistant, people were looking to me about what to do. So, I had Paul call the director. Gene's alarm clock had rung and was turned off at 5:15 am, so the call woke him. I collected three actors and drove over to pick him up. Getting into the back seat, Gene was sloshed by his milk and granola, spilled when the front seats were returned to the upright position.

A couple of blocks from the freeway my idiot temperature light went on. There was a gas station right there, thank God. So I pulled in and demonstrated my gas jockey experience in uncorking an overheated radiator. I filled the radiator but the temperature light was still on and Joaquin, an actor whose automotive expertise went past mine, told me the engine was not getting cooled at all and that I couldn't drive the car. Gene made a policy decision. We would take the Bay Area Rapid Transit Train (BART) to Fremont. Driving the mile or two to the BART station, I was smelling and hearing my engine and whining about it. The Camaro stalled at the next light and the guys pushed my car into the BART parking lot. Gene told me that I didn't have to bring the Berkeley Street Theatre plywood sign and that made me happy.

Things turned out okay. A couple of us dug out the money for the others' train fare. There had been a misunderstanding about the time of the first class for which we were to perform, so we got to perform for all four classes, even though we were late. Gene's brief talk complemented our presentations. He explained our short parables. During the lunch hour, we performed for hundreds of high school students in the plaza. A large percentage of the students were noisy and inattentive, and ten or twenty were rude—trying to break an actor's concentration by throwing pennies. But several hundreds of them made up the best audience we had that fall. They were rapt. Things went wrong when we did shows. But we took the bitter with the sweet, and got the job done. We made mistakes, accidents happened, people let us down, and the devil did not want us to perform—but God was with us.

Guidelines

There were specific guidelines that I reinforced as a director of Berkeley Street Theatre. As the director I was in charge of the play, the one who was responsible for its preparation. I had the authority to make the decisions and assumed the responsibility for them. As BST's director, I was the leader of the group. I knew basically what I wanted to say with the play. Sometimes I had the play worked out in great detail before the first rehearsal; at times, I required the actors to write the details. As a director, I came in with lots of ideas; sometimes my cast came up with more of them. The director's ability to stimulate and encourage the actors to think is important. If the director is the writer of the street theater play, he is also the editor. The director decides what will be discarded and what will be retained. If the play is too long (in street theater, this is an easy mistake to make) it is the director's fault. The perfecting of a play takes place in rehearsal. The director must assess whether or not the actors know their parts. If they are unsure in rehearsal, then the distractions on a noisy campus will make them more uncomfortable. Speaking of noisy campuses, are the actors loud enough? Are the characters believable? If they are poorly written or unbelievable, then you can't expect to touch the audience. Is the play too slow or wordy? If so, it's the director's responsibility to cut it or to get the actors to move the play faster. If the cast members do not know what they are doing, it is the responsibility of the director to teach them how to perform the play well.

Kindness is important. A good director is demanding. In the preparation of a play many mistakes must be made and corrected. You can be humorous—but don't be abusive. The actor and director are cooperators not adversaries. Be patient. Encourage the cast when they do something right. Tell them when they do something beautiful, and let them see your joy.

In a performance situation, the director serves the actors. Street theater performances hold many variables, and it is the director's job to make the actors as alert and comfortable as possible, so that they can concentrate on their parts. It is the director's responsibility to determine the time and place of the performance—when and where the actors will not be ignored, hailed upon, or drowned out by the Marine band. Mistakes are made and sometimes hardships must be weighed and endured.

The director can seek advice from the actors but he can't pass the buck. The director has to make a decision and accept the responsibility for the consequences. The actor has to do what the director says. If the director makes a mistake, it is his/her responsibility, so the actors should not concern themselves with the responsibility once the decision is made.

There were specific guidelines that I reinforced for Berkeley Street Theatre performers. The primary requisites were commitment to Christ and the group, and a desire to do good theater. If a member wasn't seriously committed to the work of Christian theater, he or she did not belong. Plugging roles with suitably talented individuals was too superficial an approach. Berkeley Street Theatre members were headed for good times as well as hard times, and as a director I recruited members who were going to stand together.

Commitment assumed, specialists make valuable members. A trained dancer can help the group get into shape and teach them how to move with precision, control, and economy. A speech major can train the group to communicate clearly (a lot of people breathe incorrectly and speak incorrectly and performing highlights lazy speech habits). Someone who has taken acting courses can help the other players with their characters. A person who knows how to achieve just the right results with makeup is valuable. Someone who can design and sew costumes is a real asset. Graphic artists come in handy. A small sign or leaflet looks a lot better when it is skillfully illustrated. In the areas of costume and graphic arts skilled friends of the group can be brought in for "contract jobs." All members of the group can be called upon to help the specialist in charge. Maybe they don't sew, but they can check the thrift stores and drive the costume mistress to the yard goods store. The members of the group build each other up. As a result, you learn more about makeup, your voice, and acting. Over the months your body is conditioned and you move better.

The commitment mentioned here translates into time. In order for there to be continuity and security within the group, members must owe the group a certain amount of time—maybe six weeks or maybe one year. An actor cannot leave the group because he has a bad day or has personal problems with another actor. If you are going to put plays together and perform them, you have to know how much time you have to work on them.

Allow an adequate, realistic time for rehearsal. If you hold a full-time job and can only rehearse on Saturdays, that means it will take you five times as long as it took those of us who did theater full time. It's likely that it will take such a group six months to have a good fifteen-minute play ready to be performed in public. That is okay. Please don't get a group together, immediately set up a performance date on a university campus, rehearse six hours every Saturday, and publicly perform a partially produced play one or two months later. Your friends will tell you how good it is "for only six rehearsals for beginners." Don't rush it: directors don't let their friends go out there and do a bad job. Wait until the later rehearsals to set reasonable dates of performance (with the understanding that you must create and work in rehearsal and that you will perform when the play is ready). The group must trust the director's judgment on the question of when that is. The director must be wise to have the pastor see a run through in order to get a more objective opinion of the group's readiness. Good theater takes time. This is true for both veterans and beginners. It took three weeks, three to four times a day, five days a week for Berkeley Street Theatre interns to work up a good twelve-minute play.

It is professionally desirable to keep the same actors for years. As you train together you become an effective theater team. As your confidence grows you can try different things and fail and accept correction. You feel comfortable with one another. However, people's lives involve more than their work in theater. People move, get married, go back to college, and get new jobs. A turnover in personnel is inevitable; as long as members have fulfilled their commitment, the director and others should not be upset when they leave. If God wants you to do theater, he gives you the people.

Actors need training and it takes place in and outside of rehearsal. Those who have studied speech, dance, and theater, help train the group as part of rehearsal. Performers should make use of outside resources: acting schools, universities, junior colleges, community recreation programs, dance schools, etc. Think about what will make you a better performer and seek out good instruction.

Observation is a part of learning. Singly and together attend movies, theater, dance, and art museums. Go to the zoo together and watch how the animals move. Watch television and listen to music together. There is much in the arts that will give you an appreciation of quality and ideas for your work in theater. You can expose one another to what is profitable.

Berkeley Street Theatre Teamwork

As artists we learned to be more prayerful, thoughtful, and intuitive as we encountered difficulties and obstacles in the creative process; and as Christians we learned to expect positive efforts to provoke resistance. When we performed, we sometimes got anti-Christian feedback on secular campuses, but we took it in stride because there was so much positive feedback and often it meant that people were actually impacted by the message of the performances. Teamwork is the actor's fulfillment of her own responsibilities—and to go beyond them when that is needed. When another actor makes a mistake you don't think about how much better that makes you look: you try to cover it up so that the play will not suffer. A member of the Berkeley Street Theatre would be sensitive and sympathetic to the problems that others would have with the work. We were eager to help one another because we understood that good theater was the result of corporate effort. Teamwork is manifested by the attitude and specific actions of the players. You create plays together, encourage one another, and help each other develop ideas. In rehearsals and performances, concentration and energy are elements of teamwork; interest and excitement are contagious. Teamwork saves performances when mistakes are made. Each actor is responsible for his own part but there are mistakes: I start off the show in the wrong place and the actors must improvise to cover for the mistake. The audience and the director usually don't notice when you cover for each other.

The Value of Constructive Criticism

CWLF members viewed Berkeley Street Theatre productions before they were performed publicly. Performing before an appreciative audience encouraged BST performers before their performance for the (friendly, hateful, and/or indifferent) public. Previews of this kind allowed CWLF members to respond to the following: was Christ honestly represented? How about His church? The world? Was the play obscure? Was it crude propaganda? Is the play ready to be seen in public? Are more rehearsals necessary? The director and the actors need honest feedback. They know what they are saying but does the audience? The director and actors live with the play for weeks and months. They are close to it and can use objective criticism from Christian pastors and congregants. They need honest encouragement as well.

If You Did Not Charge the Audience, How Did You Make a Living?

The actors were on the staff of the Berkeley Street Theatre, so we were on "support." BST staff people were paid by donation. Donors sent contributions to CWLF and designated them "for Gene Burkett" or "for Charlie Lehman" and those contributions made up our monthly checks. Some members worked part-time. The expenses of BST (gas, makeup, rent on our rehearsal hall, etc.) also had to be paid, so we asked Christian groups that invited us for thirty dollars. Some people contributed to the "general use of Berkeley Street Theatre" and this money helped us meet expenses. So, our performing was not contingent upon whether or not a Christian group could come up with thirty dollars; if they really couldn't, we performed anyhow. We expected the group that invited us to feed us (lunch if we were only there for the afternoon) and house us.

How Berkeley Street Theatre Emerged
as Christian Outreach

Christians often use art as an evangelistic firecracker. They attract people with a promised show and then they somehow use a speech to communicate the gospel clearly. These speeches carry the real content. The theater, the bait, is of secondary importance and it is often slapped together in a short period of time by well-intentioned non-artists.

In contrast to this approach, Berkeley Street Theatre worked up and performed short plays: plays that took a critical look at something common to everyone's experience (bureaucracies for example). In order to show that those who are living outside the lordship of Christ are not living the life they were created to live, we were committed to Christian art and specifically to Christian drama. We did not perform plays in order to gather a crowd and then speak to the crowd and deliver tracts.

Prayer was an important part of our work. We prayed at our daily rehearsals (we did not rehearse on the days we performed) about our personal problems and joys and about the plays on which we were working. Before our performances, we prayed that God would bring the people He wanted there and obstruct the attendance of any He did not want to see us. We asked the Holy Spirit to strike into people's hearts. Later we asked Him to remind our audiences of our shows and their message according to the audience's needs.

Conclusion

Berkeley Street Theatre was an evangelical tool that brought the Gospel to the streets in a provocative and intriguing way. The audiences were usually great. I have never felt as alive as I felt during some of those performances. I wrote this chapter to encourage readers to do street theater as Christian outreach. God bless you in that effort.

4

The Great Divorce

Susan Dockery Andrews

Left to Right: Susan Dockery, Carol Rowley, Charlie Lehman, Peggy Vanek-Titus, Keith Criss, Clancy Dunigan's arms, Gisele Perez hat, Laura Berg, and Mary (?) in "The Prodigal Son".

Susan Dockery Andrews hails from North Carolina and earned a BA in Dance from Mills College, Oakland, California and an MFA from Sarah Lawrence College, Bronxville, New York. After a stint of performing and choreographing in the New York City area, Susan moved to Greensboro, North Carolina and maintained a dance company for more than twenty years. During that time, she also served in arts administrative positions and taught in the public schools for more than fifteen years. Susan is currently married to Spencer Andrews and has two sons, Peter and Hunt, a daughter-in-law, Michelle, and two grandchildren, Jesse and Melissa.

As a CWLF street theater performing artist Susan brought grace of movement, comedy timing, and an appealing blond-haired all-American girl look to the ensemble. In her own words:

What Does the Lord Require of You? To Act Justly, to Love Mercy, and to Walk Humbly with Your God.[1]

I grew up in Greensboro, North Carolina and came of age about a mile from where four African-American college students sat at a Woolworth's lunch counter to challenge the Jim Crow laws of the day. My family attended a Presbyterian church regularly, but our church didn't seem to have much to say to the swirling social upheaval in the city. When our pastor did try to do a joint project with an African-American Presbyterian church across town, some members of our church complained and the project was abandoned. It seemed incongruous to me that the words of Jesus that I heard every Sunday did not seem to apply to the inequality and poverty that I witnessed in our city. The Quakers, however, had maintained a strong radical Christian presence in our area of North Carolina, managing an Underground Railroad way station among other subversive endeavors. I was introduced to feminism and other progressive ideas when I attended Guilford College, a Quaker school, for my first two years.

By the time I was in my senior year studying dance at Mills College in Oakland, California, I was attending CWLF's Saturday night worship at Dwight House and ready to leave the ivory tower of academia for more "real life" experiences. My radical Christian perspective started in the segregated south, strengthened in college, but certainly solidified in Berkeley.

1. Micah 6:8 NIV.

Berkeley Street Theatre was the most important part of the CWLF experience for me. Being a part of a small group that prayed, created, and performed together on a daily basis was very nurturing. Gene Burkett was sincere and honest about his relationship with God and was a very caring and patient director and leader. We respected Gene's judgment and accepted his decisions, artistic and spiritual. As we performed on UC Berkeley's Sproul Plaza or some other secular location, I became aware of the spiritual battles that were being fought to bring God's truth to non-believers. Sproul Hall and Plaza were the sites of the Free Speech Movement in the 1960s; and, after much turmoil, the area in front of Sproul Hall was designated by the UC Berkeley Chancellor as an area of open discussion for all political and religious groups. Actually, the Free Speech Movement allowed CWLF and Berkeley Street Theatre to set up and perform any day without any need for permission. On any day of a performance a clash of many groups representing various causes, political or religious, showed up and set up at tables in the Plaza. You might see Jews for Jesus or followers of Sun Myung Moon or communists or gay pride groups. Many a Hari Krishna parade, complete with orange robes, chanting, and tambourines, traversed Sproul Plaza close to our usual performing area. It was a many-ringed circus. Sproul Hall stood as a monolithic, neoclassical backdrop, a symbol of scientific and capitalist power. It's no wonder that sometimes we were assailed with negative thoughts or a lack of energy as we prepared to perform. The energy of the place was palpable and powerful, and it makes me wonder if the Plaza served as a spiritual locus for other peoples in times past. Regardless of the spiritual assaults, we hung together as a group who prayed and worked together and simply trusted each other.

The writings of Francis and Edith Schaeffer and Hans Rookmaaker of the L'Abri communities in Europe were very important to CWLF and Berkeley Street Theatre members. Most of us read at least some of their books, attended a talk by some Schaeffer relative or associate at First Presbyterian Church of Berkeley, or discussed their ideas in various settings. The Schaeffers and Hans Rookmaaker wrote extensively about the arts in relation to the Christian faith, and Rookmaaker actually visited the Bay area and took a group of CWLFers to a San Francisco museum and saw a portion of a Berkeley Street Theatre play. Unfortunately, I was not present and cannot report on the details.

Francis Schaeffer, who greatly influenced our viewpoint in the street theater company, states: "Christian art is the expression of the whole life of the whole person as a Christian. What a Christian portrays in his art is the totality of life. Art is not to be solely a vehicle for some sort of self-conscious evangelism."[2]

Street theater was a common form of political expression in those days, and I remember doing street theater with Mills College dancers in 1972 to protest the Vietnam War. San Francisco Mime Troupe was started in 1966, and I recall that we as Berkeley Street Theatre members referred to its influence. As I remember, we chose not to put Christian in the title of Berkeley Street Theatre because we felt we were reflecting the times and providing truth and insight into those times. We certainly met plenty of people in Berkeley who would write us off if they thought we were coming on too directly or emphatically with a Christian message. Director Gene Burkett often talked about our theater work as pre-evangelism because we got people questioning our culture, its ethics, media, and institutions. We felt strongly that ending with an altar call was not what we should do. After a performance we might talk to folks that came up to us and invite them to a fellowship meeting. Also, people staying at the CWLF community houses were encouraged to come to the performances and reflect on the message. We did not feel apologetic for our approach. It was something that was discussed often and agreed upon. We didn't believe we needed to portray only a biblical story and felt free to use a TV game show format or commercials or a simple medical form to create plays to relate to our audiences. As our audiences viewed some of the ridiculous subject matter in our modern lives, they could perhaps ponder the sublime and spiritual.

Francis Schaeffer stated that "A Christian should use these arts to the glory of God, not just as tracts, mind you, but as things of beauty to the praise of God. An art work can be a doxology in itself."[3] This was a great challenge. During this time, I began to wonder why it was so easy to portray destruction and negativity but much more difficult to portray the good, true, and sacred as many-faceted and full-bodied. CWLFers, myself included, were big fans of C.S. Lewis's works, and many had read all that he wrote as well as the books by his friends in the Inklings, a group of writers and believers in Oxford. In C.S. Lewis's book, *The Great Divorce*, heaven was hard, bright, and monumental compared with a greasy, translucent, shadowy Hell. Heaven was not a place of wispy clouds but a rock solid reality. I can't say that any one of our plays or performances reached "doxology"

2. Schaeffer, *A Christian View of the Bible as Truth*, 412.

3. Schaeffer, *Art and the Bible*, 10.

status, but they were complex, tightly constructed to keep the attention of the audience, and some were very humorous. Charlie Lehman as Willy Nilly in *Choose or Lose* was a hoot as he was dragged from scene to scene, a hapless victim. We all could relate to that as we laughed at Willy Nilly's plight. Willy Nilly was our version of Everyman.

In *The Hidden Art of Homemaking*, Edith Schaeffer wrote, "It is true that all men are created equal in the image of God, but Christians are supposed to be conscious of that fact, and being conscious of it should recognize that importance of living artistically, aesthetically, and creatively, as creative creatures of the Creator. If we have been created in the image of an Artist, then we should look for expressions of artistry, and be sensitive to beauty, responsive to what has been created for us."[4] She also wrote, "Food cannot take care of spiritual, psychological and emotional problems, but the feeling of being loved and cared for, the actual comfort of the beauty and flavor of food, the increase of blood sugar and physical well-being, help one to go on during the next hours better equipped to meet the problems."[5] Edith Schaeffer influenced me as a young woman hopeful of getting married and having a home. She made me realize that making a beautiful meal or cleaning a bathroom with love and thankfulness, or picking flowers for a bouquet were important and vital acts of beauty, as important as a finished dance. Anna Burkett and Bonnie Bernstein were very successful artists of the home, providing serene and lovely havens for their families. I don't know if they were conscious of Edith Schaeffer's influence, but I could see it in the beauty they produced in their homes. The community of CWLF involved women who were a bit older teaching younger women. Every time I cook a stir fry, I think of Cathy Squires, who taught me how to use whatever is in the refrigerator to make a fast and healthful meal. We learned to think of art in a broad way as it applied to the content for street theater shows, or for how we looked at housework and a modest home.

It's hard to believe that, when we lived in Berkeley, each of us paid as little as forty dollars per month for a room in one of the CWLF community houses. We had the luxury of living in one of the most beautiful metropolitan areas in the world and the ability to work five out of seven days a week on our art with other street theater members. We lived extremely simply, but we didn't need to work three jobs to be able to eat and pay our rent as many artists are forced to do today. We had the luxury of time to pray,

4. Schaeffer, *The Hidden Art of Homemaking*, 32.
5. Ibid., 124.

think, and let things cook as we developed a new show. We were able to take advantage of music and dance concerts, museums in the culture-rich Bay Area, and to read many books.

Young people who want to be artists often flock to the large, expensive cities and find themselves working many jobs to make ends meet, hoping to carve out some time to audition or take classes in their discipline. I did that in New York and finally left after six years, frustrated that I had so little to show for my efforts. A better strategy, I think, is to look for a city like Detroit that is very inexpensive and welcomes creative young people. Just walking through the light show at the Detroit airport is an inspiration and a tribute to a hope that Detroit will rebound. Or, find other people that want to make art in a rural setting. Art requires a focus that is singular, and a person may not have the stamina to thrive in her art form if she doesn't choose to live in a place where the cost of living is not so demanding.

Hans Rookmaaker states that "Art is a form of play rejoicing before the face of God."[6] What can I say? We made the attempt to be faithful to God and each other, and stay open to God's movement in our lives and art. Some days we may have approximated some success.

I adapted portions of C. S. Lewis's *The Great Divorce* in collaboration with my Berkeley Street Theatre peers. In this production there was an emphasis on the individual's choice—even from hell—to accept or reject God's love. It was a significant challenge to capture the joy and beauty of the ones who chose God and heaven, as well as the despair of the pitiable wretches who could not. I'm sure that I did not do the great and clever book justice, but it was wonderful to adapt and direct this material in a supportive environment.

In 2010 I completed the largest artistic project of my career. The production, *Standing Down the Stretch Out*, was based on an oral history found in *Such as Us: Southern Voices from the Thirties*, edited by Tom E. Terrill and Jerrold Hirsch (UNC Press). I used shadow puppets and modern dance to tell the story of James Evans, a Greensboro textile worker who started a union in 1930 in response to desperate working conditions in a cotton mill. He was a Christian who refused to have his actions dictated to him by the company-influenced pastors or mill owners. His compassion and activism necessitated much sacrifice and suffering, but he obtained peace and satisfaction even though his efforts failed. It occurred to me that this production has a direct connection to the experiences of Berkeley Street Theatre.

6. Rookmaker, *The Creative Gift*, 104.

Although personal tragedies, failures, and the press of family and work have dampened the zeal of my Berkeley days, I still see the radical Christian influence in the James Evans work and in my politics and faith. Berkeley Street Theatre and CWLF continue to have a powerful influence on me.

Resources

Susan Dockery Andrews' email address: art4all@att.net

5

Surprised by Christ

Father James Bernstein

Left to right: Arnie Bernstein and Clancy Dunigan in "Registration."

Father James (aka Arnold) Bernstein's father, Isaac, was born in 1909 in the Old City of Jerusalem. Isaac was raised to be an Orthodox Jewish Chassidic Rabbi. He lost faith as did many Jews following the Holocaust of World War II. All four of Arnie's Jewish grandparents were buried on the Mount of Olives in Jerusalem. He was born in Lansing, Michigan in 1946 and raised as a Conservative Jew in Queens, New York, where he lived for twenty-five years. During his teenage years, he won many chess titles, including amateur championships at the Marshall Chess Club in Greenwich Village, and the United States Junior Chess Championship (under sixteen years of age division). In 1967, while he was living in Israel for a year on the Israeli/Jordanian border between Jerusalem and Bethlehem, the Six Day War was fought. Following the war Arnie was one of the first to move into the Old City of Jerusalem from the New City, living with an Arabic Christian family near where his father had been born.

Arnold Bernstein graduated from Franklin K. Lane High School in Brooklyn, New York in 1964, and from Queens College of the City University of New York, with a BA in Economics in 1970. He was President of InterVarsity Christian Fellowship at Queens College in 1969 and 1970. Upon graduating from college in 1970 with a degree in economics, he moved to the San Francisco Bay Area with his Baptist pastor friend Moishe Rosen and a few others, in order to establish a brand-new ministry called "Jews for Jesus." At that time, he also became involved with the "Jesus Movement" and worked as a staff member of the Christian World Liberation Front located in Berkeley, California. This ministry was a radical street Christian ministry offshoot of Campus Crusade for Christ.

In the late 1970s, Fr. James worked in Silicon Valley as a senior production supervisor making integrated circuit "chips" while also serving as a pastor of an Evangelical Orthodox Church (a small Protestant denomination) on the path to becoming Orthodox. In 1981 he and his family were received into the canonical Orthodox Christian Church (Orthodox Church in America – O.C.A.) Four years later the Bernstein family, now expanded to six, moved to Crestwood, New York where he attended Saint Vladimir Seminary, receiving his Master of Divinity degree in 1989. His wife worked as a registered nurse and also received a Master's degree from Columbia University in midwifery. While at the seminary his friends in the Evangelical Orthodox Church movement became canonically Orthodox as they were received into the Antiochian Orthodox Archdiocese. Soon after, the Bernstein family transferred from the O.C.A. jurisdiction to the Antiochian Orthodox jurisdiction in order to be reunited with their

Evangelical Orthodox friends within the Antiochian Archdiocese. In 1988 Fr. Bernstein was ordained a priest and given the ordained name of James (named after James the Just, the brother of the Lord and first bishop of Jerusalem). He served as an assistant priest in a large Orthodox Church in Bergenfield, New Jersey. Then in the Fall of 1989, he moved to Lynnwood, Washington just north of Seattle to establish a new mission. He eventually built a church temple and it has grown into a full-fledged church. In 1997 Fr. James was made Dean of the Pacific Northwest Deanery and in 1999 was elevated to the rank of archpriest. In recent years, he has been a support for Fr. Alexander Winogradsky, an Orthodox priest of Jewish descent living in the Old City of Jerusalem where he serves Orthodox Christians of Jewish descent in Hebrew, Yiddish, and modern Russian (as well as other languages) under the Jerusalem Patriarchate. Here is his story:

As a former member, I was honored to be asked to reflect on Berkeley Street Theatre as a Christian outreach to the counterculture. Short of divine intervention, it was unlikely that I would become part of Berkeley Street Theatre. I grew up in Queens, New York in a conservative Jewish Family. Among my best friends were Tom and Frank. Both loved classical music, were Christians, and had parents who were born in Sicily. Frank, who had been reared Roman Catholic, had recently become interested in the Jehovah's Witnesses. I asked him to give me a New Testament to read, as we did not have one, and he gave me the Jehovah's Witness version. I was about sixteen years old, and, for me, receiving the New Testament—which I had always viewed as "the enemy's book" and absolutely forbidden—was scary. I read it with fear and trembling, feeling that I was committing a great, unpardonable sin, fully expecting to uncover great evil in it. I studied it in secret under the covers of my bed at night, with a flashlight. I was mesmerized by the New Testament's description of Jesus Christ. This was not at all the person I expected to find as the central figure of Christianity. I thought I would discover someone who was ruthless, intolerant, prejudiced, and even militant—a lot like a few of the Christians I knew. Instead I found a model of faith, love, wisdom, and restraint. Under intense attack, Jesus conducted Himself with what appeared to be truly supernatural grace, wisdom, and love. In the account of His life contained in the Gospels, I could not find a single event in which He behaved in any way that was less than exemplary. Then I came to the accounts of His week of passion, betrayal, and crucifixion. Of this I was certain—no one ever lived as did Jesus. I was confronted with a major decision: what to do with Christ.

The Turning Point

Wrestling with the issues of truth is no simple matter. The more I struggled, the more frustrated I became. I was entangled in a web of conflicting ideologies, and I realized that, regardless of my effort, I might not be capable of discovering the ultimate truth of knowing God. This led to serious discouragement and a sense of futility. As a young man of sixteen, I was idealistic enough not to surrender to despair—but it was not easy. Often in exasperation I would wonder: If life has no ultimate design or purpose, why continue living? I arrived at a point of crisis when my need to discover the truth of God became all-consuming. I continued to study and to win chess tournaments, and superficially appeared "normal," but underneath it all was an unseen maelstrom. Then a glimmer of hope appeared. I became aware that, though my desire for God was praiseworthy, my efforts to discover or experience Him were futile; it was not possible for me as a finite creature, through my efforts alone, to discover the eternal God. The only way I could find Him was if He first found me. My only hope was that, if I desired God enough, God in His love and mercy might reveal Himself to me. So I began praying, "God if you exist, I beg of You, reveal Yourself to me." Because I was so impressed with the Gospels and the life of Christ, I also pleaded with most desperate intensity, "Enable me to know whether Christ is true or not." For a few days I continued, in private with an abundance of tears to beseech the Creator to rescue me.

Then the totally unexpected happened. One day when I was alone in my bedroom, I very suddenly, as if from nowhere yet also from everywhere, experienced a dramatic sense of the presence of God. It was much more than an inner warmth gradually building to a point of culmination. It was more like a flash of lightening coming from the pitch-black darkest night. It was sudden and overwhelming and I felt it at the core of my being. It is not possible to describe adequately the essence of this encounter. It was the living light of the presence of God. I did not merely think—I knew it was God. I knew it as clearly as I knew my own existence and the existence of the world. The presence communicated to me directly in an indescribable way, "I Am; I exist, and I am always here with you, at all times and in all places. Do not fear; I love you and always will." These were not words that I heard, but rather the sense of what was communicated. Also revealed was that Jesus Christ and the Gospels are true. What especially made this encounter with God real for me was that I can remember a specific point in time before which I walked, as it were, in a darkness. Whatever thoughts, words, emotions, or prayers I said prior to this encounter were expressed in an atmosphere of darkness in which God was a distant possibility, not a presence. Following this dramatic encounter, the inner light went on and God became ever-present. The sense of His presence never departed and in fact remains with me to this day. I consider this to be my personal conversion to Christ. I understand that many have not had such encounters. I don't think that everyone has to have such an experience. Some are raised within the Christian Faith and at some point claim it as their own; others convert from other faiths. In both cases, often the transition is gradual and not sudden. God in His wisdom chose this particular way to reveal Himself to me. For this I will be forever grateful. But I do not expect that everyone who desires it will have the same encounter. God deals with each of us uniquely. [1]

I am a Jewish boy from Queens who found joy in a personal encounter with Jesus. In John 9: 35-38, Jesus healed a blind man who testified of the miracle to the Jewish leaders. These leaders had announced that anyone saying Jesus was the Messiah would be expelled from the synagogue. This man's faith was severely tested by some of the authorities who cursed and evicted him from the synagogue. Jesus found him and asked him if he believed in the Son of Man. He answered: "Who is he sir that I may believe in Him?" Jesus said, "You have seen him and it is he you are speaking to." The man responded, "Lord I believe" and worshiped Him. Like this blind man in John's account, my spiritual eyes were opened by Jesus and I received him as my Lord and Savior. No one can ever take away the eternal life that Jesus gave me. Persecution came when I followed Jesus. I lost friends, so it was a great blessing in my life when I found new friends who loved Jesus in Berkeley Street Theatre.

Berkeley Street Theatre

I became involved with Christian World Liberation Front through Moishe Rosen. In the Fall of 1970, Moishe and I and a few others moved from New York City to the San Francisco Bay area in order to establish a brand new ministry called Jews for Jesus. We had previously been involved with Beth Sar Shalom Ministry in Manhattan that had a unique approach to evangelism. Moishe envisioned having a more visible approach that would catch the attention of the media and make it known that there are Jews that believe in Jesus and still consider themselves to be Jewish. As part of this

1. Bernstein, *Surprised by Christ*, 31, 32.38-40, used by permission.

effort, we held demonstrations in San Francisco's North Beach, protesting the topless clubs at prime time during the weekends. We used placards and leaflets. It was a means of witnessing and also publicizing Jews for Jesus and the Jesus Movement. During this effort I came into contact with Jack Sparks and those involved in CWLF in Berkeley.

Under the leadership of Jack Sparks, CWLF engaged in a number of creative ministries, presenting the Gospel in forms and language that were understandable to the counterculture. The ministry outreach I was most involved with was street theater. Christian street theater is a form of guerrilla theater presenting a Christian message—in short, creating skits using minimal props. Among our troop of seven or so was my Queens College buddy Charlie Lehman, who as a child had been adopted by a loving German Lutheran family in Queens. He decided to join me out on the West Coast after graduating with a degree in drama. His presence on the team encouraged me and reminded me of home.

Under the direction of Frank Couch and Gene Burkett, Berkeley Street Theatre created from scratch a series of six or so skits, each lasting about ten minutes and presenting a subtle thought provoking message. We often used parables from Scriptures or elsewhere. One of my favorite skits was taken from *The Giving Tree*[2] in which the tree was presented as a metaphor for God. We linked the individual skits together in order to convey a common Christian theme, presenting aspects of Christ's life and teachings as the answer to life's greatest issues.

Our street theater troupe used no stage, amplification, sophisticated costumes, or expensive props. We performed outside wherever people congregated, with plazas and public parks our sites of preference. The troupe sought mobility, flexibility, and minimal expense, so we did not advertise or reserve sites. Guerilla theater was simply about appearing and performing. At Berkeley we performed at the free speech plaza next to Ludwig Fountain, where Jack Sparks at other times would conduct public baptisms.

In contrast to Christian performances that only used theater to bring attention to a gospel message or to give out tracks so that people would say the sinner's prayer, Berkeley Street Theatre performing artists embraced the creative arts as an evangelical tool to foster spiritual revival. The crowds at our presentations numbered in the hundreds. Those gathered were often decisively anti-Christian, making our effort especially challenging. This awareness made our presentations all the more rewarding, as in spite of our biblical Christian message we were warmly received, often with enthusiastic

2. Silverstein, *The Giving Tree*.

applause. The audience loved us in spite of our message because the skits were presented creatively with artistic excellence and respect for our audience.

Love of Beauty

Later I read a book called *The Philokalia*, which in Greek means "love of beauty." It is a collection of texts written by ascetic saints of the Eastern Orthodox Christian Church between the fourth and fifteenth centuries. These texts present the love of and desire for moral and spiritual beauty as an intrinsic, created aspect of human nature. My extrapolated understanding held that all that is truly beautiful—including good art—has inherent value and power, manifesting the creative love and beauty of God. In a sense I discovered both viewpoints to be true. All beauty comes from God and reflects His creative love, with or without the attachment of a message. On the other hand, all of creation—including beauty—serves to remind us of God. So beauty and art have both intrinsic value and the power to draw us to God.

How Berkeley Street Theatre emerged as a Christian Outreach to the Counterculture

Berkeley Street Theatre's *Choose or Lose* protagonist, Willy Nilly, has the opportunity to choose doors marked "life" or "death" in a satire of contemporary game shows. Willy Nilly is the postmodern Everyman. *Choose or Lose* was not a creed or a sermon. Instead of giving all the answers, *Choose or Lose* asked the right questions and made audiences think and feel. Because of this unique approach to its performances, Berkeley Street Theatre was able to combine improvisational scripts and street theater as a highly successful Christian outreach to the counterculture of the time.

    Contact me for support, prayer, or advice: I am available. My friend Charlie Lehman, who also contributed a chapter to this book, is a talented director, actor, and playwright. I will of course defer to him and would advise that you direct questions to him if he is available.

Resources

Father James, "Surprised by Christ" is available at: https://www.amazon.com /Surprised-Christ-Journey-Orthodox-Christianity/dp/1888212950/ref=sr_ 1_1?ie=UTF8&qid=1347743685&sr=8-1&keywords=surprised+by+christ

PART 2

Christian Guerilla
Theater Now

6

Still Small Theatre Troupe and the Place of Grassroots Christian Theater Today

JMD Myers

Left to right: JMD Myers, Eli S. Donis in *How I Met Our Father*

JMD Myers is a playwright, actor, composer, director, stage man-
ager, musician, jack of many trades, llama farmer (for serious),
proud aunt, and (when she has to) producer. She is a graduate of
Gordon College in Wenham, MA, an elder of Pilgrim Church in
Beverly, MA, and the founder of Still Small Theatre, which gets
around to all over Massachusetts.

Berkeley Street Theatre and Still Small Theatre

S till Small Theatre Troupe is a fairly recent comer on the theatrical scene,
being founded in 2012. This chapter is a follow-up report on what God
is currently doing in grassroots Christian theater ministry. There are numerous differences between Berkeley Street Theatre and Still Small Theatre,
partly because of their most important similarity: a commitment to "translate" the Gospel for our current culture. As the culture and the artistic
community have changed, theatrical approaches and trends have as well.
The spirit behind these ministries, however, is remarkably similar, spring-
ing from a deep desire to make Jesus known, and from the artistic heart
that sees art as inextricably linked with life and spirituality, rather than as
a mere tool for delivering a message. Because of that dual commitment to
doing ministry well and doing art well (which could be considered a single
commitment to telling Jesus' story well), both companies maintained/
maintain high artistic standards, a deep dependence on God's Spirit, and
a ministry approach that respects both the audience's spiritual journey and
theater's role as thought-provoker and question-raiser, rather than orator
and question-solver.

The structure and ethos of both ministries dovetails with similar cultural preferences of their day—grassroots/independent/anti-establishment
(depending on the language of the era), concerned with social justice, in
love with good art—while speaking challenging messages to their cultures,
not just parroting the culture back to itself. For both ministries, minimal-
ism has been both a practical and artistic choice that was likewise linked
to cultural preferences of the day. Berkeley Street Theatre spoke to the
counterculture of the 1970s. Still Small Theater speaks to the postmodern
millennial culture.

Beginnings

"You're crazy, but I can't think of a good reason to say no."

A number of our projects (including the initial prototype of the company itself) have started with my co-founder Eli Donis saying this to me.

We started Still Small Theatre Troupe in 2012 (after founding and running a club built on the same model during college), with a lot of prayer and quite possibly a lot of insanity. For the first eight months or so, we met every other week with interested people just to pray and seek God (and brainstorm, and laugh). Then in the fall we began to pull together a cast for our first production, *The Prophet Project*, a piece that is hard to pigeonhole into any theatrical genre, incorporating dance, movement, music, and an almost-cruel amount of memorization, all using nothing but the words of the biblical prophets for text.

And that's pretty telling of the troupe itself. We're still completely reliant on prayer. And we're still hard to fit into any niche. Most Christian theater is in sketch form (e.g., skits for Sunday mornings or youth groups), and the majority of the people doing it have no formal training. Most musicals either don't tour (because they're too unwieldy), or are huge-scale productions spun off from Broadway. Most arts groups are in constant need of funding, and frequently making requests for it. Still Small, on the other hand, tours full-length, Christ-centered productions (musical and otherwise) that are adaptable to a variety of spaces, written and directed by professionally-trained theater artists, and used to raise support and awareness for other charitable causes.

And we pray. A lot. Because so far, it's a lot better than saying no!

Still Small's Model:

Four things have been integral to the makeup of Still Small since its inception:

1. performing high-quality plays that help people connect with the heart of God,

2. holding talkbacks with our audiences after every show,

3. partnering with other charitable causes, and

4. fostering growth (spiritual and artistic) amongst our actors and other workers.

While these are the major cornerstones articulated in our mission, a few other distinctives have become part of our identity (some intentionally, and some by the Lord's surprising intention!): a minimalist approach to theater, a profound inclusivity, a collaborative approach to other ministries, and a penchant for doing things for dirt-cheap.

Commitment #1: Beholding the Lord

The importance of beholding the Lord is hard to overstate, and it's at the root of why we're doing theater at all.

The Bible talks about this consistently—from the psalmist's "I have set the Lord ever before me" to the exhortation in Hebrews to "fix your eyes on Jesus" to multiple invitations in the Gospels to "come and see." Interestingly (and I cannot at all take credit for being the first one to point this out!), most of the invitations in the Gospels were given to people who were not yet followers of Jesus. The implication, it would seem, is that beholding Jesus is powerful enough. It's not about how fervent we can remain; it's not about how well we explain the Gospel; it's not about us trying harder: seeing Jesus will be enough for us.

And that makes sense. To see Jesus is to see love; is there anything more compelling to draw people to the beauty of the Gospel? To see Jesus is to see pure goodness; is there any better way to keep ourselves pure? Seeing Jesus leads to loving Him, and seeing how He loves leads to loving others. But how do we see Him?

One of Still Small's founding concepts is the idea that, when people hear things said in the same way over and over, they become deaf to those things. Sermons have been central to the western church for a very long time—and yet it's been said that lecture (of which sermons are a type) is the least effective medium of communication. There is a large segment of the American church today that is cynical, apathetic, or both, in part because we feel like we've heard it all before. It's not that God's Word has lost any of its power, or even that people are doing a bad job preaching it, but we've heard it in the same way so often that we can't truly hear it anymore. There is a large segment outside the church, on the other hand, that hasn't heard it all before, but isn't sure they even want to hear it the first time, and are very leery of being "preached at."

And yet people both inside and outside of the church are longing for connection, with each other and with God.

Theater is uniquely suited to help meet this need for a number of reasons. (Now I need to add the disclaimer that I don't believe theater to be "the" answer to our need to see God. There are countless ways God uses to connect with us, and theater certainly does not have the corner on the market! But I do believe it to be incredibly useful, and I'll tell you why...)

First of all, let's consider the power of story. It has been said that stories are one of the most effective forms of communication—which makes it pretty unsurprising that Jesus used them so often. It seems that we're wired for story. Not only do we remember them better than lectures or even sermons (I'm guessing most people could sing me songs from *Beauty and the Beast* much more readily than they could recall the major points from a sermon on unconditional love), but we're generally more enthusiastic about listening to them in the first place (How many students have to drag themselves to a lecture? How many students have to drag themselves away from a movie?). Even more intriguing than how well we remember them, though, is how we engage with them in the first place. We interact with stories very socially, automatically applying stories to our own lives, mentally comparing people's actions to what we would have done, or considering how we would have felt in the same situation. Unlike bullet points and lectures, stories make us search for the meaning in them ourselves, which empowers us as listeners: instead of passive recipients, we're participants in the communication process.

A related and often overlooked strength of storytelling is displacement: if you want to talk about any serious issue, be that the Gospel or the environment, people get very uncomfortable if the message is explicitly directed towards them. "You need to care about this/do this/not do this/believe this/change this," makes people feel singled out and "preached at" right away; worse, it makes them feel judged right away, which puts them in a defensive posture where they're not open to respond with respectful dialogue. Why? Because they already feel disrespected.

Well-told stories bypass this problem by displacing issues into the lives of characters. The message, then, is not "look at you—you terrible audience member, you!" but "look at this person and her super-interesting life; look at the problems and issues she faces; look at how she feels about those things and deals with them (and look what a good ironing job the costumer did; she should get a raise)." Displacing issues creates space to think about them safely. Additionally, because the issues already have a human face on them, there's less of a feeling that "you're preaching at me without knowing what it's like for me." The thought and compassion required to portray a human being well necessarily mean that the issues in a character's life are not simply abstracts to the storyteller.

Another strength of theater is the ability to take an abstract concept and give us a mental image for it. We tend to be pretty visual creatures, and while we do excel at abstract thought we often don't relate with it. That's why the Bible doesn't stop with saying "God is love"[1]; it also says "There was a man who had two sons..."[2] and goes on to give us one of the most enduring images of divine love, the image of the Father welcoming the Prodigal Son back into his arms. It's why God didn't stop with saying "[I am] the Lord, the compassionate and gracious God . . . forgiving wickedness, rebellion, and sin"[3]; He also said (and I am paraphrasing here!) "Hosea, go marry a hooker who is completely horrible to you, take her back and love her just as much after she cheats on you, and then tell the world that this is the way I'm going to forgive them." God is not abstract, and God's love is not abstract, but we often use abstract language in order to be able to talk about it at all. (Case in point: the word "love" itself is technically an abstract noun—when not used as a verb of course—and the previous sentence would have made no sense without it.) Theater and storytelling let us move from (very important and necessary) conceptual understandings to expressions that can hit us on a heart level.

The ability to hit on a heart level has always been of great importance, because however often we've tried to deny it and claim that we operate by reason alone, human beings are very "feely" creatures, and are swayed by how we feel about a person or a subject far more than most of us would like to admit. It may, however, be of even greater importance in our current twenty-first-century culture because of our lack of grounding in absolutes. We are no longer a culture that primarily believes that truth is knowable and universal—and that therefore, if you believe something, you should have sound reasons to back it up—but, instead, a culture that believes that all points of view are valid, and that therefore the only thing you need backing up your beliefs is that you feel that way or that it "works for you." While we still honor science and long for things that we can prove, "the buck stops" in our culture not with reason, but with individual feeling.

1. 1 Jn 4:8b, NIV.
2. Lk 15:11b, NIV.
3. Ex 34:6b-7a.

I am not here to talk about whether this cultural shift is a good thing or a bad thing, but to talk about how it underscores the need for theater in our culture today. Theater lets us connect with characters (and by extension, the issues they deal with and abstract concepts they embody) on an emotional level, in a culture that longs for connection and venerates feeling. This ability to stir the emotions is heightened when music is involved; I won't get into the science behind it right now, but suffice it to say there is a strong biopsychological connection between emotion and music. People are hardly exaggerating when they use words like "magic" in relation to the emotional impact of music; most neuroscience seems a little magical when you get into it because the Lord made the brain so incredibly complex, dynamic, and fascinating. Music and theater grab people by the heart in a way that very few other things do.

Finally, theater helps us to stand on our heads. Many art instructors recommend that, in order to learn to draw accurately, one ought to look at the subject upside down (not necessarily through standing on one's head, although that would be an entertaining way to do it). The reason is that we're so used to seeing things right side up that, instead of seeing the shapes and lines that make them up, we tend to see them as a whole and draw the image that is ingrained in our minds, not the image we actually see. Looking at something upside down breaks us out of the image that we're used to so that we can actually see it. In the same way, looking at God through the lens of theater can break us out of the patterns of seeing Him that we're so used to—the phrases that have become trite or pat, the right rote answers, the words we no longer process when we hear them—and lets us look at Him again.

Now, when I was in college, I met with a lot of skepticism about my desire to do theater that explicitly dealt with the Gospel and other spiritual matters. The dominant sentiment was "do plays that have meaningful themes but don't mention God, and people will still get good things out of it without being turned off." The discomfort was understandable: these were people who had by and large grown up in Christian homes and whose experience of the interplay between Christianity and theater consisted either of being told that the "secular" plays they wanted to do were immoral, or of being shoehorned into very poorly done "Christian" skits and plays. There was a lot of discussion in classes about what it truly meant for a play to be "Christian" and support of the value of doing plays that touched on deep truths without explicitly tying them to Jesus.

I have a lot of respect for my colleagues from that theater department, and for the deeply meaningful theater that we all produced together, very little of which was explicitly "Christian." I think the plays we did then, and the plays a lot of them do now, are incredibly valuable, and I agree very much with their essential point: that just because a play doesn't say "Jesus" doesn't mean it lacks the Gospel message. (For instance, *The Winter's Tale*, by William Shakespeare, deals deeply with themes of grace and redemption and even alludes to resurrection, all from within an imagined ancient pagan context, and, while it does not explicitly mention Christianity, the parallels to the Gospel are remarkable.) In fact, personally I tend to be the sort who can see echoes of the Gospel in just about anything.

But our presuppositions have a lot to do with what we glean out of a story, and the Gospel parallels that jump out at me in the story of *Sleeping Beauty* or *Romeo and Juliet* wouldn't usually occur to someone who isn't already coming from a Christian perspective. So the situation is a little bit akin to general revelation: Paul points out in Romans 1 that God's nature is visible in the natural world,[4] but then continues in chapter 10 that people actually need to actually hear the specifics of the Gospel in order to truly connect with God.[5] I believe that every culture has been prepared by the Lord through its stories and customs to understand the Gospel, but it is usually not until He sends someone to use those inroads to explain the Gospel that they become clear. And so while there is certainly a place for "non-explicit" (for lack of a better term) theater, it may not be as effective in bringing up important spiritual truths as some would like to claim—at least not without a friend taking the opportunity to discuss those buried truths with the viewer. (It's also worth noting that most of my colleagues at the time did not sense a personal call to evangelism or ministry; their calling in life and intention in theater are very different than mine, and perfectly legitimate.)

Their concerns about cheesiness and manipulation in "explicit" theater are also legitimate and worth mentioning. It seems that just about any time people are passionate about a message (whether Christian or not), they run the risk of having their message overwhelm their art. Not to pick on Upton Sinclair, but *The Jungle* is a good example of this. He was so passionate about "evangelizing" about Socialism in his book that his story became very manipulative—the main character suffers terribly until discovering

4. Rom 1:19-20.
5. Rom 10:13-15.

Socialism and then suddenly, everything is rosy; Sinclair frequently lost the real humanity of his characters in his concern to make his point. Incidentally, the book arguably had a much bigger impact on the nation's food safety regulations than it did on the nation's views on Socialism, causing Sinclair to lament, "I aimed for America's heart and hit it in the stomach." This is very frequently a problem in "Christian" theater, to the point where I too am often nervous and skeptical when I hear about it (and often end up cringing at least once while watching it). But this doesn't mean that "explicit" theater shouldn't be done, or that it is doomed to be something people sit through politely and uncomfortably. Actually, it means we need to be more passionate about our message.

If we really care about our message, we'll be careful to make the best use possible of our medium for telling it. When we care about it superficially, it's easy to get caught up in the abstract concept of it—for instance, it's easy just to cut and paste the words we've always used to explain the Gospel into the characters' dialogue, instead of considering how they would interact with the Gospel and each other and their deep needs. This, of course, loses all of the benefits of standing on our heads and giving people images and all the other great strengths of theater that we discussed above. If we truly care about what we're talking about, then we care about how it plays out in the real world. More to the point, if we truly care about the Gospel and the love of God, then we will love the characters and audience members as He does, which means that we will care about our characters and their lives enough to tell their stories well and not lose their humanity, and we'll care about our audience members enough to tell stories in a way they can receive. "Explicit" theater can and should be done; it just needs to be done with excellence.

These are the philosophies behind the first tenet of our mission. Doing artistically excellent theater that is specifically Christ-centered combines one of theater's greatest strengths—the ability to get people willingly engaging, thinking, and feeling—with one of the biggest needs of our culture: connection with God.

Commitment #2: Talkbacks

Our second commitment grew out of my time at Gordon College. The fantastic theater professors there, Jeff Miller and Norm Jones, often held a talkback after one or two performances of each show (which usually ran for nine performances total). It was fascinating as an artist to get to talk with an audience after a show and hear what they'd personally gleaned from the show. It was also fascinating as an audience member to ask questions and gain greater insight into how the director and actors had been thinking about the show and growing through it in the long rehearsal process. I got to see how much more meaningful a show became when audience and artists were given this time to process it together. Because Still Small is particularly ministry-oriented, we especially wanted to give people this time to unpack the show, ask questions, and delve deeper into the themes it addresses. All of the talkbacks are optional—we certainly don't want to force "meaningfulness" on people, especially given many people's fears about "Christian theater" bashing people over the head—and we give people a moment to exit if they don't want to or can't stay, but usually well over half of the audience stays to talk. Time and time again, we are blessed and blown away by the insights audience members bring, the conversations we have with them, and the ways they report being touched by the performance.

Practically speaking, having a talkback helps people absorb what they've just seen. Our culture doesn't leave a lot of space for reflection, and often people don't get the chance to process a show without that intentional space made. It also gives us an opportunity to answer questions that come up for people—and hopefully it helps hosting ministries keep an eye out for people who want to dig deeper and need support in that. The other, not-as-expected, outcome is one that has me very excited for the potential growth of the church: it contributes to fellowship among audience members. Christians are called to love each other as family, but between the highly busy schedule of the average twenty-first-century human and the frequent setup of Sunday morning church (spectator-style and sermon-oriented, followed by scattered casual conversations in a large space not conducive to intimate interaction), we have to be very intentional about developing relationships with each other if we want it to happen. Plays followed by talkbacks allow people to share a leisure experience and then share their thoughts with each other at an unusual depth, because the environment created by a theater talkback invites and treats as safe a level of thoughtfulness that is, in many other contexts, unnatural.

Commitment #3: Charitable Partnerships

The third tenet of our mission was inspired by history. Starting in the 1500s and lasting for nearly three hundred years, the revenue from theatrical productions was used to support the hospitals of Madrid, Spain.[6] I was fascinated by this: today, most arts organizations ask for money to further their work (often after they've already charged at the door!). Not only that, but there are more and more nonprofits being created every year, all of which are also asking for funding (frequently for causes that are arguably much more urgent than theater). Is it possible that theater could contribute to meeting the needs in the world, rather than adding to them?

The short answer is yes. It requires certain sacrifices, such as doing theater cheaply—but, then again, theater can be done a lot more cheaply than many people realize. More importantly, theater can contribute awareness.

What we do at Still Small is to pair each show with a cause that is in some way related to the show's theme. (We get this approved by our board, of course, making sure that it is an organization that is trustworthy, financially responsible, and in line with Christian values.) So, when performing *The Prophet Project*, which brings to life the words of the ancient Hebrew prophets, we took a cue from the prophets' dual commitment to social justice and the knowledge of God, and we teamed up with Gospel for Asia's Bridge of Hope program, which breaks the cycle of poverty by providing education for low caste children while also teaching them (and, by extension, their families and sometimes whole villages) about the love of Jesus Christ. With *The Diary of Perpetua*, which is adapted from the prison diary of an early martyr, the connection to the work of The Voice of the Martyrs was obvious. *How I Met Our Father*, our comedy on coming to faith, had a lot of room for creativity, since it interweaves many diverse stories. Partly because of its personal, down-to-earth feel, it has often supported more local causes, such as Beverly Bootstraps, a north-of-Boston-area food pantry and center for empowering the economically disadvantaged, or Amirah Boston, an agency providing after-care to trafficked women. Now that this show is in repertory (available year-round), there is also an option for hosting ministries to use it as a fundraiser for their own work.

In all of these situations, the monetary amount that we're able to give to the cause is limited, but the impact that we have by boosting its visibility is far greater than a dollar amount. (And, really, for any charity event, the

---

6. Brockett, *History of the Theater*, 148-50.

money raised is only a small part of the purpose—it's just as much about raising enthusiasm, understanding, and potential new supporters, all of which arguably last longer than the financial boost.) With theater, there's the added benefit of connecting the cause with what the audience was just watching and feeling. One of a charity's biggest tasks is putting a human face on its cause so that people truly understand the "why" of the mission and can get behind it on a heart level. That significant challenge is met by the nature of the pairing of a show's theme with the charity's mission.

This is not to say that we're trying to get every audience member deeply involved in every cause with which we partner. But for the few people in the crowd whom God has prepared to be deeply involved, it may be a life-changing introduction to that cause; for the people already involved, it's a welcome encouragement, and for those whom God has called elsewhere, they not only get to hear about good things going on, but they also get the satisfaction of knowing that they contributed at least once through their admission donation, even though they can't be involved on a regular basis.

Commitment #4: Ongoing Learning

So, here's a conundrum: because of the nature of acting and the demands of the craft, actors are trained to be as emotionally vulnerable as possible; because of the nature of the theater and film industries, an actor who wants work has to continually put him or herself in situations that are very likely to end in rejection. Strip away as much mental armor as possible, and then fire at will upon the ego: who thought this was a good idea? Most actors live life in near-constant instability (for instance, there is never a guarantee that, after one project ends, you'll get another one), and this is not healthy for anyone, let alone the highly sensitive types that tend to gravitate towards acting.

In addition to this, the industry's casting process actually works against the craft itself. Dustin Hoffman pointed this out in an interview about the movie *Tootsie*: Good acting comes out of studying a character extensively, and thinking deeply about and preparing oneself for the role, but an audition only lets a director see what an actor comes up with in a few minutes. Basically, they're left trying to judge a person's acting ability without letting them actually engage in the discipline of acting. It has also been my experience that actors thrive on being stretched and being cast in a variety of different roles; most audition processes never let a director see an actor's versatility in order to make those creative casting choices that bring energy to a production and growth to the actor.

What if, instead, an actor got to work with the same group of people for an extended period of time, long enough to know each other's strengths and build on them? What if there wasn't always such a risk of being rejected every time a new show came along? The actor would get to focus on doing excellent work, rather than always having to fight for the chance to do it. (I am again indebted to the inspiration of others here, including some of director Anne Bogart's writings about her work with the SITI company.)[7]

In any case, these were some of the ideas that went into creating the very supportive atmosphere that is Still Small. There is also the principle, of course, of "use it or lose it," which applies to just about any discipline, including acting and Christianity. I wanted to make sure that we as a company never lost skill as actors nor focus on Jesus, and so we've built in from the beginning a commitment to ongoing learning and development, both as actors and as Christians.

A lot of this happens very naturally. Any director doing his or her job will help actors to grow, simply by pushing them to excel in the roles they're rehearsing. And it's nigh on impossible to get through table work (the part of the rehearsal process where you sit down and analyze the show and its meaning, the characters and their personalities and decisions, the relationship dynamics, etc.) without having it affect your personal spiritual life, especially when working on plays that handle spiritual matters as overtly as ours do.

We're also, however, very intentional about making time for artistic and spiritual development within our rehearsal process. Whether it's work on improvisation, music, or physical and vocal differentiation of characters, actor training is built into rehearsal, usually in a way that directly complements the needs of that particular show. (For instance, we had a friend with an extensive dance background lead a workshop for our actors in *The Prophet Project*, which made heavy use of stylized movement; for *How I Met Our Father*, which was written by the cast, it was more important to focus on improvisation exercises to keep everyone in a highly creative

---

7. SITI (The Saratoga International Theater Institute) Company is an ensemble-based theater company whose three ongoing components are the creation of new work, the training of young theater artists, and a commitment to international collaboration. SITI was founded in 1992 by Anne Bogart and Tadashi Suzuki to redefine and revitalize contemporary theater in the United States through an emphasis on international cultural exchange and collaboration. http://siti.org/content/about-us.

mindset.) Similarly, our spiritual disciplines and exercises are often related to the play. For *The Prophet Project*, we read, prayed over, and discussed not only passages from the prophetic books of the Bible, but also passages from A.J. Heschel's illuminating work *The Prophets*. For *The Diary of Perpetua*, we had countless discussions of what following Jesus looks like in our own context, read numerous passages from Christians under persecution, prayed in a wide variety of styles, read some of Jesus's own words about persecution, and listened to the Lord about His love. In keeping with the way the Lord has formed the identity of this company, we also begin and end every rehearsal in prayer.

It isn't always easy for a director to make time for these things—at least not without a fair amount of anxiety about what else might not be getting done—but we schedule it in nonetheless, because we're conscious of our need for them. It is consistently powerful to seek God together with people who have not only a common faith, but also a common task. Not only that, but we recognize the fact that if we're not keeping our eyes on Jesus, there's no reason for us to be rehearsing in the first place. And we're usually in desperate need of prayer for one reason or another.

A Few Other Things That Happened to Become Part of Us

Several other things have become part of our identity, whether by practicality, planning, or Providence.

Our fairly minimalist approach to theater is in part because of the logistics of traveling. When you're packing everything—set, props, costumes, lighting, actors, and in some cases the actors' overnight bags—into two or three cars, it's very helpful if you don't have a large, extravagant set and a plethora of props and costumes. Touring also means that we're constantly adapting our shows to different spaces, which is made easier by using simple set pieces that can be placed a little closer together in this space, a little farther apart in that one—and squished depth-wise, but expanded width-wise, for that one oddly shaped room. To give a sense of what I mean by "minimalist," we have never used more for our set than a black back curtain about twelve feet across (which we don't always use, depending on the show), and three black "rehearsal blocks": wooden cubes measuring roughly eighteen inches (which we don't always use either). That doesn't mean our shows are visually boring—they're usually quite lively and colorful—but all of the necessary props and costumes usually fit inside a single rehearsal block.[8] Because of my concern for us to be a help and not a drain, our bare-bones approach is also partly a matter of financial practicality. However, a lot of it also stems from watching theater in college, and realizing that the fewer "trappings" a performance had, the more attention was put upon the actors' performance. It can be breathtaking to watch a lone black-clad actor deliver a monologue on an empty stage—and it can be hilarious and engaging to watch simple blocks be used as church pews, cars, chairs, coffee tables, beds, and walkers for chattering elderly ladies, all in the course of one show.

Still Small's radical inclusivity won the Eldin Villafañe Award for High Distinction in Christian Service from the Center for Urban Ministerial Education (CUME) of Gordon-Conwell Theological Seminary, Boston Campus, and was almost entirely God's fault. We certainly valued diversity already, but the often-unlikely actors that perform in our shows aren't there because we were on a social inclusivity crusade; they're there because we need them. It can be hard to find people who are willing to commit the incalculable amount of time and energy that acting in a show requires; ask people to participate in a Christian show and your pool of potential actors is even smaller. And so we were a little surprised when our casting received appreciation for integrating people from very different socioeconomic backgrounds, denominational backgrounds, and races/ethnicities. Sure, we'd laughed about how God had brought together former addicts, local college students (one of whom was majoring in computer science, not theater), a Harvard-trained lawyer, and a llama-farmer, who were variously from Trinidad, New Orleans, New York, and New England, but it hadn't seemed profound at the time: they were simply the friends we'd been able to rope into doing the show. In fact, we almost didn't recognize the description of drawing actors from "the low-income housing project across the street," because that somehow sounded like we were being magnanimous towards them, when really it was the other way around. As it turns out, this casting diversity has been a very healing thing for some people, especially for those with disabilities (autism spectrum disorders, ADD, etc.), who have frequently found themselves excluded from other groups and activities in life. These people are often our most dedicated workers. Our casting is still pretty much a matter of using whatever and whomever the Lord gives us,

8. A rehearsal block is a large box that can be used as a prop on stage, but also can be used to store props and costumes for a play.

but we're more appreciative now of the wider things God wants to do by bringing together hilariously different people.

Ministry partnerships are also an important part of our model. This, again, is largely for practical reasons: by virtue of being a touring company, we're not around for follow-up. And, while the Lord can certainly use anything He likes in people's journeys towards Him, we weren't comfortable with the idea of "hit-and-run ministry." It seemed much more effective to partner with existing ministries—churches, campus ministries, etc.—to complement and build on the work they are already doing. This also means that there is somewhat of a built-in audience: people are much more likely to respond to an invitation from a friend than they are to a generic advertisement, and the fact that these ministries are already established in their communities means they have many more connections in their areas than we would. Not only that, but partnering with a ministry means that we have free access (for churches, because they own their own buildings; for campus ministries, because they have official status on campus) to what is usually one of a theater company's biggest expenses: performance space. On the other side of this equation, holding an event like a play can be a great way for a ministry to gain more visibility, so that more people are drawn into contact with it, and a great way to reach out to segments of the population who are terrified of "church," but love art. We're excited to see more and more of the ways God wants to combine the many diverse gifts of different groups to build up the Church and bless the world.

Working with a Group of Christian Artists:

The experience of working with a group of Christian artists is unique. We were somewhat prepared for the need to be patient with each other, submit to each other, work through problems—in short, we were prepared for it to be hard. I don't think we were at all prepared for it to be this good.

In the past I had not come across other activities where there was this combination of shared depth and shared purpose. Frequently, Christians have opportunities for shared depth—for instance, Bible studies (although even then the depth depends on people's willingness to share and to delve into things)—but no task, goal, or anything that draws the group outside of itself or its routine. Conversely, there are numerous opportunities to serve—at soup kitchens and food pantries, even sometimes on VBS and worship teams—where the task takes all of people's attention and there is no opportunity for delving into our relationships with each other or with God.

I did not realize how powerful it was for those two elements to be combined until we started doing it. Here was a place in which—partly because of the nature of the craft and partly because of the design of the company—we were delving deeply into Scripture, our own humanity, our thoughts and questions about God, and our lives as Christians, while at the same time working together to prepare something that would minister to a wider group of people. Not only that, but we were having fun together—an easy element to overlook in trying to build Christian community, because it's not inherently "spiritual." However, it is an incredibly important part of building a group that actually enjoys one another's company, which, when you think about it, ought to be an element of truly being the family of God. One of our policies as a company is to schedule individual "exit interviews" with each participant after a show, so that our leadership can be aware of any problems that need to be addressed, any ideas or experiences from which we can learn, etc. One of the things that I heard again and again in interviews after that first show—and have continued to hear many times since—is that this work has been one of the most powerful experiences in people's spiritual lives.

This was a big part of the reason that we started offering classes. We realized that with as much as our audiences were getting out of performances, we were getting exponentially more out of working on the shows. We wanted to open up that opportunity to more people, and now offer a six-session introductory course on using theater as a spiritual exercise, which can be scheduled at the convenience of churches or other groups.

Of course, this doesn't mean that it hasn't been hard, but the difficulties have lain not so much in interpersonal problems (which so far have been rare, and quickly healed by God's grace), but in what we're pretty sure is spiritual warfare. All sorts of things go wrong—and I mean badly wrong, like losing actors days before a show, or twenty minutes before a performance, due to circumstances outside of our control such as injuries or severe car trouble. But this has also served to deepen our faith and our fellowship, as we've needed to rely on the Lord together and depend on each other. In fact, this last element—shared adversity—is said to be the strongest relationship-builder out there, and has been an oddly important part of our lives together.

Waking the Sleeping Princess: The Need for Theater

Interestingly enough, the handsome prince did not go into Sleeping Beauty's tower, smack her upside the head, and say "Wake up, you goofball! What were you thinking, touching that spindle and going to sleep for a hundred years?!" Maybe she deserved it, and who knows if it would have been effective, but that's not what he did.

We're often tempted to do something similar, though. After all, human beings have turned away from their Creator and need to be awakened to their need for Him—and it's easy to assume that an urgent situation necessitates an urgent, loud manner. And let's face it: The Church has issues. It's easy to see our sins and failings and want to smack someone, or shout until something changes. (At least, I often feel that way; maybe that's my own sins and failings coming to the fore.) Now, it may be that there is a place for strong words, when the Holy Spirit prompts them. For Still Small, however, it seems that God has put us in a position of kissing the sleeping princess awake.

The Disempowered Church and the Use of Theater

One of the Church's biggest testimonies of God's grace to the world is the fact that we're not perfect. The blessing-side of our tendency to fail, sin, and make mistakes is the way that God's mercy restores us, the opportunities it gives us to exercise forgiveness by His power, and the way it shows the world that it's not about our goodness but His. It also means, however, that the Church will always have various foibles that need to be addressed (and that theater will always have a useful role to play in bringing us back to the truth.)

I am not here to enumerate what those issues are. However, I am very interested in how the nature of theater (as opposed to specific plays' subject matter) may be used by God to address a few current trends in the American Church.

With the caveats in place that this statement is a generalization and an opinion and is untested by the FDA, the American Church is hugely disempowered. We're still trying to get over the historical clergy/laity divide, which means that we still tend to believe the responsibility for most things in our churches—whether events such as prayer meetings or responsibilities such as discipling young believers—lies with those who are in full-time ministry. Not only is this an easy attitude to have because of our "consumer culture," but it's unintentionally reinforced by a lot of the ways in which we "do church." Consider the experience of the average evangelical churchgoer: he or she enters a worship service on Sunday morning, sings a number of songs that were written by others, selected by others, and are being led by others (often with amplification that drowns most of the congregational singing), listens as someone else prays, and then sits and (hopefully) listens while someone else reads the Word of God and expounds upon it, prays again, and gives a benediction. To what extent can this even be called participation? And, if this is someone's primary means of Christian fellowship, when does he or she ever experience the truth that he or she is a vital, beloved, necessary part of the Body of Christ, with unique gifts that no one else can bring to the table? There is also a fair amount of ignorance in the American Church, despite the fact that we have access to copious amounts of scholarly materials and Bible translations. However, if people are not connected to the fact that they have a vital role to play in the life of the Church and the service of the world, what reason do they have to educate themselves?

(Time for another disclaimer: theater is not the answer. Anything that is not Jesus is never the answer. But Jesus is using theater.)

One of theater's gifts to the disempowered church is its demand that the audience participates. Movies control everything the viewer sees and leave very little up to the imagination; lectures and sermons do the interpreting for the audience and require only that they absorb the message (or in the worst case, only that they don't make noise if they fall asleep). Theater, however, leaves quite a lot of "gaps" that the audience has to fill in imaginatively: it is perfectly suited to what the mind does naturally. It also requires the audience to tease out the meaning in the piece, which requires much more mental engagement than listening to being told what the meaning is by someone else.

Another gift, albeit one that is experienced more richly by the participants than by the audience, is the way theater can be used as a tool for spiritual growth. In the first Encountering God Through Theatre course that I taught, I was particularly touched by the enthusiastic response of one of our participants, for whom the character research for the final presentation (a reading of an Easter-themed play) was some of the first Bible reading she had done, despite having attended church for years. This participant consistently mentioned how much she was learning—and how much she was enjoying learning. Similarly, I was delighted in a post-show interview with one of our regular actors to hear her say that she never thought she wanted to be a missionary, but that she was now recognizing our work as mission work and loving it. In both cases, it wasn't that someone said "you should be doing this" or "you should be interested in this"; it was the natural outgrowth of seeking God through theater that was a rich encounter with Him.

Theater also creates a much needed space for relationship formation. I don't mean to say that Christians aren't already forming relationships with each other, but—again, as a generalization—Sunday services are often not the best environment to foster interpersonal depth. There is very little opportunity for interaction during the service, and almost no privacy for interactions after the service, which makes it very easy to simply have multiple shallow interactions and then go home. We need time with each other besides just Sunday mornings, and theater is available as one means of making that time. Those who work on a play share a large amount of time characterized by shared purpose, fun, vulnerability, and hardship, and leads to strong, intimate relationships. Those who come to see the play experience a smaller amount of time spent in shared enjoyment—also a necessary component of healthy relationships—as well as a forum for discussion and reflection.

As we continue to grow and connect with more places, I am looking forward to how theater may contribute to empowerment in the Church by its availability as a ministry tool. Pastors are usually swamped with demands on their time and attention—but one of the great things about theater that can tour easily is that it doesn't need to be commissioned, scheduled, or supervised by a pastor. As long as he or she receives approval from the necessary decision-makers (depending on a church's constitution, this may be the elder board, a pastor, the mastermind who keeps the church calendar, or someone else), any layperson can bring a play to his or her church with about as much effort as it would take to organize a potluck (and without having to wipe punch off the floor or make sure that there are fewer than five bowls of potato salad). This means that, if an "ordinary" churchgoer decides she wants to bring in a play, she probably can—and she won't be overwhelmed or under-equipped in doing so. Not only that, but a diverse array of gifts—prayer, evangelism, listening and encouraging, etc.—can flourish and be used in follow-up afterwards, meaning that just about any Christian who wants to get involved can do so, without having to be responsible for the whole event. Indeed, I've often thought that our touring plays can be as much of a ministry opportunity as people want them to be, able to use as much or as little participation as people want to put in. (Perhaps this is the spiritual dimension of the old theater adage that theater will take everything you put into it.) Without creating a dire need for volunteers or service hours, hosting a play opens up opportunities for a lot of "ordinary" Christians to use their gifts.

Arts and the Twenty-First Century:
Theater Outside the Church

I mentioned it earlier, but it bears repeating: the arts are a heart language of our culture. A while back, I came to the conclusion that, if you're funny enough or if your music is good enough, people will let you say anything—and they'll enjoy it! Consider *Les Miserables*—the entire story turns on one man's conversion story. Take away Jesus, and you don't have Valjean. And yet the play is hugely popular and has run for decades. People who are resistant to religion don't have a problem with *Les Mis*, because it's a compelling story with memorable characters and beautiful music.

It has also been mentioned (by the dramatist Jeffrey Sweet[9] and probably by others) that twenty-first century Americans get a lot more of their ideas about the world from entertainment than we realize. His example was a courtroom: most of us have a very clear picture of what a courtroom looks like, complete with who sits where. Far fewer of us have actually been inside of a courtroom, and, for those who haven't, chances are that mental picture came from TV and movies. If entertainment is influential enough that it is our source of mental images of tangible, physical things, it stands to reason that it also has a significant effect on our ideas about more important things such as spiritual realities. There are statistics upon statistics about how much film the average American watches, but the bottom line is: it's a lot. Because it's a leisure activity, we don't have the same defenses up that we have in other parts of life, and so we more readily absorb the images and ideas coming from what we see, rather than critically evaluating them as we might if the same ideas were presented in, say, an editorial. (This is the concept behind product placement!) Arts and entertainment are things we readily let into our hearts and minds. I say this not to encourage some sort

9. Sweet, *The Dramatist's Toolkit*, Chapter 14.

of manipulative use of the arts (all too tempting for many of us who realize the power of our medium!), but to point out the extent to which the arts are a heart language of our culture.

A few interactions have affected my perspective on using theater to bring the Gospel to the world. One was a conversation with an InterVarsity worker who was kind enough to sit down with me to discuss the potential for theater to be an outreach tool in local campus ministry. I sensed a little skepticism on his part about using theater in ministry because the evangelism training he'd received (and the general strategy of InterVarsity) emphasized the need for first building trusting relationships between Christians and non-Christians, rather than preaching to strangers and expecting conversions. This was another reminder to speak the language of the people we're trying to reach: in American culture (and New England, where I minister, particularly), tent revivals don't work very well. The name of Jesus is not so completely unknown here that handing someone a tract or simply telling the Gospel—techniques that are hugely effective in some cultures—piques a person's interest the way they do elsewhere. This doesn't mean that we shouldn't expect results from doing Christ-centered theater (or that we should put God in a box regarding how He may want to work!), but it helps a little to clarify what we're doing. Given the culture in which we're operating, our plays are not likely for many people to be the tipping point into a conversion experience. But they may be very useful as a step on the journey: they may be one of many pieces of the puzzle of seeing who God is, they may provide trust-building experiences for those who have not had respectful interactions with Christians before, and they may be very effective as ways to enter into the conversation about God (a necessary prerequisite to the "conclusion" of conversion). And, while it is true that a trusting relationship with a Christ-follower is often a crucial part of a person's coming-to-faith journey, it's also true that a lot of Christians feel very uncomfortable starting spiritual conversations with their non-Christian friends; having a concrete shared experience such as a play to talk about may help people bridge that gap between caring deeply about their friends and actually talking with them about Jesus. (This is another example of the helpful role of displacement: "let's talk about that play" is a lot less threatening, for both parties, than "let's talk about you and JESUS!")

The other interaction was an anecdote from a non-Christian acquaintance about how uncomfortable she'd felt when a stranger tried to share the Gospel with her. As sad as it made me, it also made me realize that there is a place (and need) for less-direct evangelism. I recognized that, had I been in her shoes, I would have felt the same way because I hate conflict. If there is a subject on which I might disagree with someone, I'm terribly uncomfortable discussing it with them; I would much rather investigate it on my own time and have a safe space to figure out what I think, rather than trying to figure out what I think while feeling strong social pressure to get along and agree. At the very next meeting with our core administrative group, I brought up the subject of "introvert evangelism": how to offer information about God, while respecting people's different processing needs and styles. We came up with a few strategies at that meeting: printing the web address for a site like Cru.org (which offers resources for people interested in Christianity, while giving them the option to contact staff to ask questions or be left entirely alone while they investigate) on the backs of our paper tickets, along with our own website and the website of the charity supported by the show, gives people an easy way to get more information on any of those three things, without being "in-your-face" about it or requiring them to pick up a pamphlet or information sheet (or be seen by their friends picking up information about the Gospel—a very real consideration for some people). Refraining from putting out evangelistic materials on our information tables (usually reserved for information about the show, the selected charity, and the troupe) keeps people from feeling like they were "tricked" into coming to an evangelistic event, or that they were only truly welcome at our shows if they were ready to consider the Gospel. We make it clear during our talkbacks that we're available to talk further one-on-one and that we're happy to talk to people about God, but we do not do a public "altar call" (although we do sometimes offer prayer). These are not hard-and-fast rules, and our approach may be tweaked a little depending on the play or the environment in which we're performing, but, in general, we try to respect the complete terror with which most people regard attempts to "convert them," and we recognize that the role God has given us is more "conversation starter" than "conversion clincher." For some, not being "preached at" may be the only way they're able to be open to the message. It may be harder to measure success when God has called us to be a step in the journey rather than the end of the road, but we would rather respect the culture and needs of the people to whom we're ministering, and trust God to bring the fruit (whether we ever see it or not), than impose our own ideas or human traditions about what evangelism should look like.

God has also placed some surprising inroads for our broader culture within some of our plays, and I am fascinated to see how these play out more in the future. The example that comes immediately to mind is *The Diary of Perpetua*. This play is based on a document that is over eighteen hundred years old: the prison diary of a young mother martyred by the Roman authorities for her unwavering commitment to Jesus. Hugely significant for the study of women's history, this document is one of the oldest female-authored documents known to history. Not only that, but the woman in question didn't just write down her own story. In society in which a father's word was final, a citizen's ultimate loyalty was to the emperor, and a woman's place was squarely in the home, Perpetua went against her father's wishes and defied just about every expectation for a woman in her society as she lived out her ultimate allegiance to Christ. I knew almost none of this when I sat down to adapt her diary into a play. But God's plans are much broader than we expect, and now we have a play that is relevant to women's history/gender studies, African studies (Perpetua lived and died in Carthage, which is in modern-day Tunisia), and human rights studies—all of which are very "in" subjects these days—in addition to its relevance to Roman history, Church history, modern persecution, and theater itself (the repertory production employs character doubling and other stylization in a way that makes it of interest to certain segments of the artistic community). In addition, some of the philosophical and relational elements of her story fit surprisingly well into modern predilections: Perpetua stands up for what she believes in, she revolts against society and against her parents' wishes, she's braver than her brother (a plus for a culture that promotes "girl-power") . . . and there's a dragon (also oddly popular these days). I was amazed when I realized just how many ways Perpetua's story seems almost tailor-made for our culture—and, again, this was completely unintended when we began working on the piece. Perpetua's faith is unavoidable—like Jean Valjean in *Les Mis*, she has no story if she does not have Jesus. But I'm hoping that, like *Les Mis*, our music is good enough, the characters are lovable enough, and (in Perpetua's case) the many cultural inroads are compelling enough that this show can reach a lot of people who would otherwise balk at talking about God.

If we care about the people with whom we're sharing Jesus, we will translate the Gospel into their language. And it seems that, increasingly, the language of our culture is relationship, art, music, and dialogue (as opposed to earlier languages of reason, debate, oration, etc.). It is exciting to be part of using theater to engage the world on its own terms in order to help "kiss the sleeping princess awake."

A Last Word or Two:

As our name implies, we are—well, still small. We're still a very young company with a lot of growing, developing, and learning to do, and we always try to return to being still and small before the Lord. As you feel led, we humbly appreciate your prayers for God's use of us and for those who will come after us. Praise God for the crazy things He does!

Resources:

If you're interested in learning more about our work, catching a performance, or possibly even joining the craziness, you can find us online at www.stillsmalltheatre.com or by email at sstt@stillsmalltheatre.com.

7

The Passion Play

Joanne Petronella

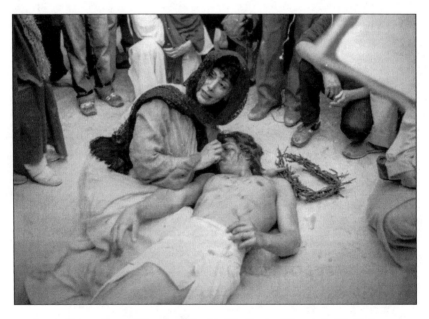

Joanne Petronella and Timothy Ballard in *The Passion Play* on the Via Dolorosa

Joanne Petronella is the founder of Christ in You the Hope of Glory International Ministry based in Anaheim, California. For thirty years, her international ministry has brought many to Jesus, reaching the poorest of the poor in India, doing ministry in the Middle East, and ministering to several heads of state. As a member of the Vatican Board of Charismatic Catholics, Joanne attended a private audience with Saint John Paul II and worked closely with Saint Mother Teresa of Calcutta. Her early ministry training was under the anointing of famed televangelist Kathryn Kuhlman. Jan and Paul Crouch's Trinity Broadcasting Network featured her cooking show, *In the Kitchen with Mama Joanne*. She was also a guest of Paul Crouch on *Behind the Scenes*, discussing her ministry in the Middle East, as well as a guest on *Praise the Lord* with Dwight Thompson, sharing about her ministry in India. Harry John, Miller Brewery heir and founder of Heart of the Nation Catholic television network, endorsed Joanne's ministry. Michael P. Grace II of Grace Motion Pictures and Charlene Eber of Hollywood Video Ventures, board members of World Alliance for Peace, produced videos of her international ministry teams in India, Singapore, and the Philippines. Joanne received three Angel Awards from Excellence in Media for bringing Christ's message to the media.

Joanne holds a doctorate in theology and founded an institute of ministry. She has authored the following books: *Deliverance from Fear, How to Lead Someone to Jesus, Disappointments Transformed into Victory, Exceedingly Great and Precious Promises with Effectual Prayer, Touch the Hem of His Garment, Litany to the Divine Lamb of Love*, and *A Manual for Ministers*. She is currently writing a book entitled *Breaking the Bondages of Witchcraft*. Here is her story.[1]

How Improvisation and Street Theater Emerged as Christian Outreach on the Via Dolorosa

As founder of Christ in You the Hope of Glory International Ministry, I directed and acted in a Good Friday street theater performance of the Passion of Christ on the Via Dolorosa in Jerusalem for over thirty years. Each Good Friday, the ministry team walked the ancient stones of the Way of Sorrows to acknowledge Jesus' death and resurrection as the key to salvation. Members of the ministry team from Southern California traveled to

---

1. DeFazio and Spencer, *Redeeming the Screens*, 135-36. "Used by permission of Wipf and Stock Publishers." www.wipfandstock.com.

the Via Dolorosa, donned costumes and make-up, and used their performing talents to re-enact Jesus' final walk.

Our street theater reenactment of the Passion of Jesus called viewers
to the foot of the cross. Onlookers responded to the agony of Jesus (por-
trayed by a young actor carrying a wooden cross) and were reminded that
Jesus' stripes and precious blood saved humankind from the consequences
of sin. Our players brought the message of Jesus as the Lord and Savior
whose death on the cross at Calvary and resurrection gave humankind re-
newed access to the Heavenly Father and to the empowerment in the Holy
Spirit. Cameras flashed as onlookers viewed Jesus carrying the cross and
were reminded of his redemptive love.

I am participating in this dialogue to encourage all those in ministry
to use their performing skills to bring the message of Jesus to the streets.
Looking back, I realized that Christ in You the Hope of Glory's Good
Friday reenactment built community among the onlookers in a powerful way. The tone was solemn, and the presence of Jesus was evident and
often accompanied by the aroma of the Rose of Sharon from the Garden
of Gethsemane (a mystical reminder of Jesus's precious blood poured out
to redeem humankind). The response to the Good Friday performance
was solemn. Strangers' awareness of Jesus' presence drew them together.
They responded to one another with the awareness that Jesus died for
them. Emotions were evident as Jesus touched each heart with his love.
My ministry traveled eagerly to Jerusalem each year, training the team in
improvisation and street theater technique to re-enact Jesus' final steps. The
team prayed in costume for the hearts that would be touched by Jesus and
receive him along those ancient stones. Team members shared hotel rooms
and returned from the performance with a certain experience of touching
hearts for Jesus. Street theater on the Via Dolorosa brought the performers
together with a certainty that they were fulfilling the great commission to
bring the lost to Jesus in a creative and compelling way.[2]

Resources

Joanne Petronella's books are also translated into Croatian and can be pur-
chased by emailing thegreenolivetree@yahoo.com. To view her television
program, visit thecrosstv.com. To invite Joanne to minister or to speak at
an event, please email thegreenolivetree@yahoo.com.

2. DeFazio and Lathrop eds., *Creative Ways to Build Christian Community*, 15-16.

8

Hollywood Outreach

Jozy Pollock

Jozy Pollock and Liberace

Jozy Pollock was Britain's "Hula Hoop Queen,"[1] but her career came to a halt when she married the famous magician Channing Pollock. She appeared on the Ed Sullivan Show and performed in Las Vegas as Channing's assistant. After accepting Jesus as Lord and Savior, Jozy gave up a life of glamour and volunteered with the prison chaplain services at East Lake Juvenile Hall in downtown Los Angeles. She became the first Protestant female chaplain at Los Angeles Men's Central Jail. Noelle Aimee Kozoll directed a documentary about Jozy's years in prison ministry entitled *On Faith Alone: The Jozy Pollock Story*. Throughout her life, she has met and befriended celebrities and understands from personal experience that many celebrities do not have the peace and love that comes from having a personal relationship with God. Here is her story.[2]

How Improvisation and Street Theater Emerged as Christian Outreach to the Hollywood Street Scene

I was born in London, surviving a World War II childhood experience of air raids, bomb shelters, food rationing, and traumatic search lights to become the UK's Hula Hoop Queen. I married the world-famous magician Channing Pollock, appearing worldwide as his assistant in night clubs and most notably at the Hollywood Palace and on *The Ed Sullivan Show*. As a divorcee in Hollywood, I became celebrated mingling with the rich and famous in Hollywood's fast lane.

Jesus' everlasting arms of love embraced me in 1982. After I experienced a romantic breakup, a friend who had recovered from an addictive life style led me in the sinner's prayer to Jesus' love and mercy and the personal peace I was desperately seeking for in all the wrong places. I am participating in this dialogue because as Paul in Ephesians 5:6 explains: "I awoke from a spiritual sleep, rose from a spiritual death and Jesus love and mercy gave me light." Acts 26:18 became the mantra of my personal experience: my eyes were opened I turned from darkness to light and from the power of Satan to God. I received forgiveness for my sins and was given a place among God's people set apart by faith in Jesus.

---

1. Jozy was famous in newspapers and in magazines demonstrating the hula hoop. She is on the cover of the Hula Hoop sheet song music.

2. DeFazio and Spencer, *Redeeming the Screens*, 63. "Used by permission of Wipf and Stock Publishers. www.wipfandstock.com."

The Hiding Place Drama Team

I had been a performer and actress in a glamorous world before my Christian conversion. Following my conversion, the Holy Spirit used my acting talent and passion to bring those on the streets of Hollywood to Jesus. In 1982, I attended the Hiding Place Church. A musician named Henry Cutrona was the pastor and Todd Fisher, the son of Debbie Reynolds and Eddie Fisher, was the assistant pastor at the Hiding Place. The church was full of beautiful people, many in the entertainment industry. I felt very much at home there because of my background in acting and modeling, as well as my experience playing theaters and casinos as a magician's assistant. A lady in the church named Diana Hood put out a call for people in the church to perform in a street theater ministry. This sounded like it was right up my alley. I knew I was an evangelist so being able to act to bring people to Jesus was a perfect fit for me.

Diana had a list of skits performed by Youth with a Mission. One of my favorites was one in which I appeared as a chicken doing the clucking sounds and waving my arms and giving various reasons why I was a chicken—just as people give various reasons why they are Christian but never walk the walk. We performed on Hollywood Boulevard in conjunction with the Holy Ghost Repair Service, which was run by a recently widowed lady named Judy. She preached to drunks and punks and she inspired me to become a preacher. Judy was tough and would not stand for any nonsense but she was very loving (Judy later married Ron Radachy and their ministry, *The Oasis*, is on Ivar Street in Hollywood). After the performances, everyone got food but first they fed on the Word of God. One night, I led a punk to the Lord; immediately afterwards one of his friends beat him up for converting to Christianity. It was a spiritual war out there on Hollywood Boulevard. Some of the Jesus People like Bobby Chance and Clayton Goligher were around. These two mighty men of God still have great outreach ministries.

One night, the Hiding Place Church took over Hollywood Boulevard with a band on a flatbed truck. That was the night I saw a demon possessed man delivered. He had come up to us with a face contorted with hate and yelled that he wanted to kill us. A bunch of people jumped into action praying and rebuking evil spirits. I was a bit nervous as this was new to me, but I was very impressed with Jane Booke (who is now a top fashion designer) who just went to town on him. Eventually, he fell to the ground and after much prayer, his face totally changed from an expression of hate to love.

He received Jesus as his Lord and Savior. It was a great lesson for me to see firsthand the power of prayer in the name and the blood of Jesus. Another lady named Nancy Hughes who had just got out of prison called for volunteers for prison ministry. I thought it would be a good idea to take the drama team into the facilities. However, God had another plan and turned me into a preacher in the LA Jail System.

I agreed to contribute my story to this book to encourage Christian performers to use their God given gifts to reach the lost for Jesus in this short time before his glorious and imminent return. God used my talents when I outreached in street theater performances bringing the message of Jesus's redemptive love to the Hollywood street scene of the 1980s. God protected me so that I am still alive today to share this testimony. Jesus suffered and rose from the dead as a light to Jews and Gentiles alike so that I could become a witness to Him as a performer. To the worldly materialistic minds of my former friends in the glitterati, it seemed insane for me to walk away from a life with the famous and fortunate to gain what seems to be so little. But Paul risked his life for a message that was offensive to the Jews and unbelievable to the Gentiles. Jesus received the same response to his message (Mark 3:21; John 10:20). As I followed Jesus, I discovered that my most prized worldly possessions were meaningless compared to even the smallest eternal reward I will receive because I performed for God's glory on those Hollywood streets.

Resources

I am available for speaking engagements. You can view my interviews online:

- *On Faith Alone: The Jozy Pollock Story*, directed by Noelle Aimee Kozoll. youtube.com/watch? v=auNvGVfes5U.

- Sheri Pedigo, "Jozy Pollock Interview on Clemente Movie, Manson, and Magic," *Live on the Red Carpet*. youtube.com/watch? v=8KhI2Yh3VrE.

- Lee Benton, producer of *Victory Road*, "The Cross TV, interviews Jozy Pollock." youtube.com/watch? v=ATHHLa86Akw.

- Lee Benton's CBS studio meetings, guest speaker, Jozy Pollock. youtube.com/watch? v=EJHNBivDUTE.

- Contact me by email for speaking engagements or interviews: haleluiaholywood@aol.com.

9

Estuary Ministries

Olga Soler

Olga Soler is director/writer and performer for Estuary Ministries, a Christ-centered performing arts ministry dealing with biblical themes, inner healing, abuse, and addictive problems. The art forms used include drama, dance, storytelling, mime, comedy, graphic arts, writing, film, and song. Olga attended the High School of Performing Arts (Fame), the Lee Strasberg Theater Institute, and the Herbert Berghof Studios, all in New York City. She has performed widely at conferences, churches, prisons, coffeehouses, support groups, youth groups, and retreats, and has even performed on the streets, at secular colleges, and in worship services across the United States and the United Kingdom. She holds degrees in education and communications with equivalent studies in theology and psychology. She studied for two years at Gordon- Conwell Theological Seminary. Olga has designed and conducted the workshops "Dance Alive" and "Trauma Drama" at many Christian Recovery conferences. She wrote the curriculum and conducted Discovery Groups for addicts at the Boston Rescue Mission, using the arts to help them process aspects of their recovery. She also conducts workshops for Christian drama and dance in many churches of all denominations. Using Paulo Freire's "Pedagogy of the Oppressed," she wrote a script for the "Mosaics" group. The "Mosaics" consists of parents helping their children—who were victims of sexual abuse—through the courts system; Olga also assisted them in filming the script for a documentary. She performed and coauthored scripts for four years with the "Team" Christian ministry in Massachusetts and conducted eight full-scale multimedia presentations out of the Rio Ondo Arts Place in Woburn, Massachusetts, including *Voice of the Martyrs*, *Techno Easter*, and *Clean Comedy Night*. She has directed and choreographed entire productions at universities and colleges, including *A Man for All Seasons*, *Jane Eyre*, *Amahl and the Night Visitors*, and (by permission of the author) Calvin Miller's *The Singer*. She has conducted retreats for women using the book accompanied by dramatic presentation. She is the author of other books and assorted screenplays. Olga is the proud mother of three wonderful children Cielo, Reva, and Ransom. She lives in Massachusetts with her husband Chris and her Japanese Chin (dog), Kiji. Here is her story.[1]

---

1. DeFazio and Spencer, *Creative Ways*, 86-88.

Acting and the Church

I came to Jesus through a church that was very much against the arts. This was very hard for me because I am terminally "right brained." That means I am one of those creative types who can't think a conventional thought to save my life. Linear thinkers make fun of right-brained thinkers for our spelling and our way of looking at things differently—but what would the world be without art? Just think about it. Even the Shakers who are the conservatives of conservatives express themselves in crafting beautiful furniture and in dance. The church I started my walk in, by the way, has changed its views on the arts considerably. I hope I had something to do with that.

I am in this dialogue about the arts because I was in the professional theater. I started drawing under the chairs in the dining room when I was a kid because my single mom could not afford to get me paper. I was the only one of five hundred students from the Bronx that made it to Performing Arts High School for Freshman Drama in 1967. Later I attended Lee Strasberg Theater Institute and "hit the boards." Art was my life, but Christ became more precious to me than art and I was told creativity was naughty. Not knowing the scriptures, I believed it. So I laid it down. For ten long years I tried to be something I wasn't. Then the Lord had pity on me and told me the truth. Art (and yes that includes even dance and acting) has been with the people of God from the very beginning.

Storytelling particularly, of which acting is an offshoot, has been with humanity since the very beginning of people groups. Believers first shared the tales of Genesis through oral tradition in so efficient a manner that versions of it have been found in the original characters of the Chinese language[2] and in many ancient cultures throughout the world. Stories were used by the rabbis (Jesus included) and the whole service of the Tabernacle was one of the greatest and longest running performances of the plan of salvation. Passion plays and mummers have told Christ's story through the Middle Ages and now we see the great conflict between good and evil told on the screen with symbolic epics like "The Lord of the Rings."

How else would we know history and how would we explain spiritual things without stories? It is impossible. History is in fact his-story or the story of Humanity. When believers tell that story we can tell it from before the beginning of time and we can also tell what will happen after the end of all things because we tell the story with God in it.

2. Kang and Nelson, *The Discovery of Genesis.*

Since a story is just an ellipse or pertinent portion of life, storytellers know that a straight narrative is not enough to get the gist of what happened, much less explain deep concepts. Symbols must be used because symbols, like pictures, are worth a thousand words. When Jesus talked about a seed as a spiritual truth in the heart he was not saying we plant a kernel of corn in our cardinal muscle. He was using a symbol with profound significance. Our internal lives as well as our dreams and hopes are all best described in symbols that encapsulate and abbreviate the realities we experience and share. How these stories affect those who listen has to do with whether we engage with them or not. If the Spirit of God has anything to do with it a connection will be made, however unlikely that may be on the natural level.

In Framingham, Massachusetts I performed for a ministry to street people where it was hard to keep the audience from participating in the performance. One time I used the story of "The Red Dancing Slippers"[3] to illustrate the folly of addiction and the power of God to heal. It was well received and I went home that night wondering what lasting impact the show might have had. A few weeks later I returned to support other performers and an extraordinary woman approached me. She was very tall and her hair was a wild orange color. Her nails and lips were brilliant red and her eyes heavily adorned with green. She wore lots of leather and large jewelry. She was just a little intimidating.

She pointed a long red fingernail at me and loudly exclaimed, "You!"

I took a step back with apprehension trying to remember if I knew this person or might have done something to offend her. Then she continued.

"You was here a few weeks ago wasn't you? And you did this thing. This thing with the red shoes . . . " I stood there thunderstruck: she remembered the story. She continued saying, "I was moved, very moved." Then she sauntered away. I guess that was among one of the best compliments I ever received. I would not have thought anything would move such a woman but the story did. I hope it moved her closer to the Lord. She came back for more so maybe that is just what happened.

One person acting or telling a story is good but it can also be done collectively in a play by a group of people. Drama, comedy, puppetry, dance, mime, and film further illuminate the parables, allegories, and skits we can share. These can all captivate an audience's attention and help people

3. *The Red Shoes* is a fairy tale by Hans Christian Andersen about a girl whose vanity condemns her to wear red dancing slippers continually until they take on a life of their own and destroy her.

identify with characters and understand concepts in a deeper way. When stories are enacted they live again and again: an artistic resurrection.

All art forms deepen the effectiveness of storytelling. The more senses employed in perceiving a story the deeper the effect. Music, props, visual effects, costumes, even smells and sounds all help impress the story into our minds. This can be good if the story is truthful and edifying, or bad if the story is deceptive or evil. It works this way because acting and storytelling, like all art forms, are neutral mediums. They are not good or bad in themselves. The rightness or wrongness of the medium depends on the heart of the one who uses them.

In the history of the church, objections to acting have been many. It is deceptive or "not real"; it is egocentric; it is worldly. This is concrete thinking at its worst—the kind of thinking that discounts a line of literature because it has a metaphor, or the worth of a master work of painting because it is not historically or physically accurate. The work of an impressionist may not look like a photograph but that does not discount its beauty or value. It speaks of reality in a different way, using emotion and color rather than concrete objects.

It is true that when we listen to a story we must suspend our unbelief and accept inaccuracies. We must do this in order to receive the message. However, in exchange for a literal account that would take as long as the event itself to tell, we get deeper realities in the symbolic encapsulated form. Abbreviation and enactment do not mean a story is necessarily deceptive. It is merely sharing a truth from another angle or another perspective. Those who have trouble with perspective need to remember that the slight differences in the four Gospels are due to the four authors' perspectives—not deception.

The objections I've heard church people make to drama might or might not apply, depending on the writer or performer. We must not let this cause us to go to extremes in accepting or rejecting the whole art form. Preaching or oratory is also an art form. It can also be deceptive, egocentric, and worldly. It depends on the one preaching doesn't it? We should not "throw the baby out with the bathwater" just because an art medium has been used badly. It can also be used wonderfully if the artist is true.

Since art and stories deal with symbols, they speak to the senses not just the mind. They can penetrate the defenses of the mind, with something that one cannot just dismiss. If it's a good story that raises questions, then one must cogitate upon it and grapple with it. It comes back to us when we are not thinking about it and, like a mental puzzle, it must be resolved. That is why Jesus did not explain his parables to most people. He did offer explanations to his disciples but not to the crowds because he wanted them to think about his stories.

Film increases the intensity of the telling because so many visual, auditory, and dramatic stimuli are used. A story told in a live play has its own intensity because the players are alive and so are closer to our person. More intense still is street theater that interacts with us and draws us into its sphere. The body language and closeness engage us like nothing else can. This is why live storytelling will never be replaced by film, however artful. Storytelling has its own unique power. It stimulates a conversation where emotions engage and soul truths can be revealed. People avoid conversations like that because they are slowly forgetting how to engage with each other and be human. With our stories we must remind them.

Can a story overcome evil? It certainly can. Our own stories of how we engaged with Christ are called testimonies. A young man named Daniel once told me, "They can argue with our theology but not with our stories. That is something we are the most expert in because we know what happened better than anyone else." In the book of Revelation, we are told,

> Now have come the salvation and the power and the kingdom of
> our God, and the authority of his Christ. For the accuser of our
> brothers, who accuses them before our God day and night, has
> been hurled down. They overcame him by the blood of the Lamb
> and by the word of their testimony. (Rev 12:10-11 NIV)

Our stories are powerful enough to put the devil down because they prove that Christ still lives—in us.

In my own story I spent the first ten years of my believing experience alienated from the arts. I do not now resent my time away. God had a very good reason for taking me away from them. With the Lord there is no waste, especially of time. We see this in the years Abraham waited for his son, the slavery years of Joseph, and the forty years Moses tended sheep. We even see it in the flight of David from Saul before he was crowned king and certainly we see it in the twenty-nine years before Christ's ministry. God waits, but while he does he is doing an essential work within his servants. While I do not compare myself to those great people of faith I do appreciate all the Lord did in me while I "languished" outside of the arts.

The arts are emotive, and taking bits of ourselves to express something is a very personal process. So artists who do not believe in Christ tend to be egocentric: it is all about them. For the believer this has to change. The way God deals with this was exhibited in microcosm on the day of my conversion. I took a break from the professional theater in New York to follow a friend to a Christian college in Tennessee. I thought I would do the tour for fun and then run back home to continue my career—but God had other plans. An elderly professor at the college by the name of Robert Francis got my attention. He had been an attorney but had turned to the ministry. However, he did not lose any of his power of persuasion. I pressed him with difficult questions but he was up for the challenge. My intellect was struggling hard against the Lord but this brilliant man was showing me that faith has genuine evidence in reality. Still, I was fascinated but not convinced.

Then I attended a service at a very conservative church that forcefully turned me around the corner. Most of the services in this place made me snooze but that day a man was speaking who had been jailed for murder. I thought this black man who had been in a southern prison probably was tougher than anyone I had seen on the streets of New York—but all that raw power was pouring out of his mouth instead of his fists and it was all for Jesus.

Keep in mind, I was still an actor and I had done some modeling. My appearance was very important to me. I was devastated by the loss of a finger nail or the appearance of a pimple. This church was also big on appearances. It was full of very wealthy, stuffy people in front of whom it was a faux pas to sniffle during service much less say "Amen." We were all projecting reserve but the man up front was holding nothing back. I started to feel this. In fact, all these explosive things began to go off inside. I did not want to lose my cool but something powerful was taking over. I can still hear the speaker saying, "I was a filthy, dirty, nasty sinner but the Lord Jesus had pity on my soul and saved me from myself!" Oh God, it still gives me the shivers. I was undone. I wanted that. I would have given anything in that moment to get it. That conviction, that assurance, that unequivocal and undying forgiveness won at such a great cost, that monstrous unyielding love. In that moment the whole building full of over two thousand people afraid to even sniffle disappeared from my consciousness. I saw only the podium where I would get the relief I needed. I was so weakened by the Spirit moving me that I fell to my knees from which I could not rise. I was dressed very nicely and normally would have been embarrassed in the extreme but in that moment I did not care. I could not walk so I crawled—all the way up to the front while indignant eyes followed me. I staggered up to the gentleman speaking. He did not appear to be surprised at my behavior but who continued to call others to the foot of the cross. Not many came, and certainly those who did walked. However, although I had to live with that moment in the eyes of the congregation that hosted the college, I consented to attend that church forever after and it was worth it. I had my prize and any humiliation I had to endure to keep it was a bargain.

Egotism is not exclusive to artists but as I said artists without Christ tend to be egocentric. Egocentricity and the selfless faith of Christ are mutually exclusive. God made me an artist. He needed to get rid of the selfishness and ego. He is still working on that but I am fighting him less and less regarding that subject. He wants us to be our best selves and ego ruins that process. I think this truth is sinking in for me and it makes the pruning easier to bear.

I was lonely and felt misunderstood for my quirkiness, but God does not host pity parties. We see this in his treatment of Elijah, who complained twice about his lonely estate. The Lord waved the complaints away with more instructions for Elijah's mission, and then added this as an afterthought: "I have reserved for myself 7000 who have not bowed the knee to Baal" (I Kings 19:18). He is compassionate after all and he does meet our real needs but we must await his timing.

In my case God showed his mercy by letting me contribute to the pro arts dialogue in the denomination of my rebirth. At first I did it in order to be accepted for who I was. That did not seem to work, especially after the spectacle of my conversion, but the Lord used my waiting time to help me get a few degrees under my belt so I could be a better person and a better tool in His hands. I studied theology, psychology, and education and got degrees in those areas. Since I had renounced the corruption of the professional theater I was glad that I now had the skills for a day job.

In time, when the Lord felt I had purged enough of the world out of my soul, He began to send real believers that were hidden artists in the church my way. I also met those who were openly creative in other denominations. That was so wonderful; like Elijah with the school of the prophets, I felt as if I had found a few of the seven thousand. Many (not all) of the artists I met, who are committed to Christ, were a wondrous breed. They had brilliant spiritual perception and were a delight to fellowship with. I thought that if the saints are the real bricks and mortar of the church then the believing artists must be the fragile but transparent windows. Miracles tended to follow them and life gained a new excitement. In England, where

I went to do mission work, I began to perform musically. Then I was led to Texas where music and puppetry, comedy and drama turned into "Midnight Oil"—my first theater company. That ministry was beset with one miracle after another as we prayed for people who were cured of drug addiction, temptation to suicide, and cancer. I first started to see the healing power of sacred art at that time. God was punctuating his work in us as artists with an infusion of grace into human pain to heal and help. We took this as confirmation that we were doing His will and it made the opposition from many quarters bearable. We were doing what we were meant to do. Then the Lord led me to Massachusetts.

If you ever hear me speak, whatever my theme, you will eventually hear me turn to the subject of community. God is doing something right now concerning the structure of His Body. We have been plodding along as a social club when we are to be so much more. We are soon going to witness greater moves in the function of the church as a unified loving community than we have seen since the first church. It may take persecution to bring it but I hope it doesn't. One way or the other the Lord will make a welcome to accommodate the upcoming harvest. I believe this will happen and I believe in sacred community because I have experienced it.

We had a believing musician's community in England and the TEAM drama ministry became my community of faith in MA. I met Vinyl Ride Out (TEAM director) during a street performance. Mad man that he is—I first saw him riding a tiny tricycle on the sidewalk as part of the show. When he stood up I was amazed at his flexibility for he was not a short man. He was also not short on creativity. Though he tended to drive his people into the ground with commitments his heart was for the gospel and he did offer us a precious and innovative opportunity for intimate and loving Christ-centered community. All denominations were represented in the TEAM and for the most part that was not a problem. We all loved Christ and we all loved each other. I now began to see another need for the church to embrace the arts besides accepting me. The church needed the arts because artists saw the need for each other. They understood community.

In addition to its healing power and its emphasis on and understanding of community, a third reason for including the arts in the church was to open its doors to more people like me. The body of Christ will lack no gift until the end of time.[4] That is God's promise. When I first became involved

---

4. "Therefore you do not lack any spiritual gift as you eagerly wait for our Lord Jesus Christ to be revealed." (1 Cor 1:7)

in church, the church everywhere needed an infusion of innovators. Many people in the arts were being demonized by church people because these artists thought "outside of the box." Such thinking made them suspect and untrustworthy in the minds of many. Sin is not however the exclusive domain of those who are "different." All people sin, but "out of the box" thinking was and is needed alongside orthodoxy because this produces the holy flexibility needed to move with the Spirit. Without it we tend to resist God when he does a "new" or "surprising" thing. God is the creator and His style has unending diversity. Though His ways are eternal and consistent in character His style is ever new and mysterious. We cannot cage Him because He will always break out. We cannot predict Him unless He reveals his plans to us. To receive His new direction, we must be open—if we are too guarded we will miss it. So, you see, the human innovator and the guardians of the faith need each other to perform God's ultimate will.

Contemporary use of the arts in the modern church also emerged alongside of the hope for the "latter rain" or the outpouring of the Spirit in the latter days. During this time, as we are told in Joel 2, the Spirit of prophesy would be poured out upon all flesh and as the veil between our world and God's realm thinned miracles would follow. The arts, if you follow them in the scriptures, were used a great deal in prophesy. Some passages of the Old Testament, such as the Psalms, are put to music; if you note the way prophesy is written in the scriptures you will see that it is formatted as poetry. Ezekiel enacted the siege of Jerusalem, and Miriam and David danced and sang. Bezaliel crafted the props for the drama of the tabernacle and Elisha used a minstrel to prophesy. The Lord Jesus and his disciples used the powerful art medium of parables and storytelling, and the catacombs of the early church were covered in holy graphic arts. Art was everywhere in the story of the church and served to illuminate prophesy. Why wouldn't it continue to do so? God calls us to "be filled with the Spirit, speaking to one another with psalms, hymns, and songs from the Spirit. Sing and make music from your heart to the Lord" (Eph 5:19). Worldly prophets are inspired by their "muses" (spirits); our "Muse" is the Spirit of the Living God.

Prophesy depends on God and so does prophetic art. Street theater may have a broad outline but it has been my experience that since the audience is unpredictable and vital the performance has to be as well. It is therefore, largely dependent on improvisation. When a believer performs or creates he or she depends on the Lord—and much more so when we have to improvise. We must move by the inspiration of the Spirit for regular art, but we also have time to rehearse and plan. When we improvise we depend totally on the Lord. In fact, many believing artists are moving more and more into improvisational art through which the Lord can function more freely. This may be a vehicle for the Spirit as predicted in Joel. Whether it is or is not—God, help us to be faithful. When He speaks, may he use us body, mind, and spirit as He will.

Healing is another aspect of the arts that is very valuable. Healing for the mind requires removing the pain from within and placing it where we can see it and process it. The talking cure works well in some respects but we also need a forum for the purging of our painful emotion. Art is well suited to this as many expressive therapists will tell you—and even more so when accompanied by a spiritual component. I began using therapeutic arts with people and created a workshop called "Trauma Drama," which participants voted the most encouraging workshop in my conferences from coast to coast. Trauma Drama was also a hit at the Boston Rescue Mission where I worked with addicted and homeless populations. It was similar to street theater in that we never really knew what to expect. The Lord knew and He worked all that out.

I have done theater in the street for the political leftist revolution of the 1960s, and for the Lord. When I did it before I became a believer I saw people scared and uncertain as they watched because they were not sure what was real or what was pretend. When I did street theater for the Lord I saw people engaged with intensity that normally would not give a preacher the time of day. I saw them stop in their business suits or in their motorcycle gear and watch as the Spirit drew them into the tale and they would not turn away. I am certain this kind of theater will never die no matter how many special effects we see in movies. It is such a wonderful tool. I have found myself acting out stories in front of teens who I thought would walk away or boo. They never did. Instead they asked for more. Once, on the Boston Common, I thought I would be upstaged by a Hari Krishna parade that was passing on the street behind me with a thirty-foot idol made of diaphanous saffron undulating material. It was quite a spectacle but my audience just glanced at it and then kept watching my story unfold. Stories, like the Spirit, will not let you go. And when the Spirit is involved, the stories engage us and hold on.

The street players in this book got out and did what God wanted them to do. The church will one day thank them for it. I have been told by bankers and hookers that what I did moved them. We can't let something that strong go unused.

The fact is that storytelling and acting, like all art forms, are powerful mediums of communication. It is our job to communicate the story of the Gospel any way we can. It is also a fact that the enemy of our souls does not want this to happen. We should ask ourselves if he is involved in the suppression of these powerful forms of communication rather than accuse others of evil in using them. This is especially true when the enemy is using these intently effective mediums elsewhere to promote fear and lies. God who is the creator certainly uses as many creative means of spreading light as are available. Those who criticize the use of arts in the church may want to remember the story of David and Michal his wife who became barren and unproductive after she criticized her husband's expression of dance before the Lord. We would not want to become unproductive as a church by ungratefully or unwisely stifling the gifts God has given us.

Resources

Olga's book *Tough Inspirations from the Weeping Prophet* is available on Amazon. If you would like support or advice as you outreach as a Christian theater troupe text or call Olga at 774-262-3815 or email her at fleursavage@yahoo.com.

10

Pensacola Outreach

Sheri Pedigo

Sheri Pedigo is a horse activist who has also produced events dedicated to "saving K-9 lives." A prolific songwriter, she provided two songs, "Caravan" and "I Find You," for James Kleinert's television documentary *Horse Medicine*. Sheri has written songs for the reality show *Blind Date*, and, in Europe, she had a hit single on the dance charts with "Caravan," which was the theme song for the Cannes Film Festival red carpet in 2010. Sheri was the opening act for country singer Randy Travis at William Shatner's Hollywood Charity Horse Show, held in Burbank, California. She has shared the stage with many musical icons, such as Toto's lead singer Bobby Kimball, Spencer Davis, Patti LaBelle, the Temptations, and Martha Reeves and the Vandellas, to name a few. Her duet with Eric Van Aro, "Born Again," was up for a Grammy in the jazz category in 2014. Here is her story.[1]

How Improvisation Emerged as Christian Outreach in Pensacola, Florida

I grew up in Glasgow, Kentucky—a town of about twenty thousand. My parents had three children, and I am the middle child. My dad always had his own business as a mechanic working on race cars. He gave everyone who came along a job. He was a giving, wonderful man. I started playing piano at the age of eight. I taught myself harmonies from old hymnals, and I made up songs with my own chords on the piano because I could not read music. I created my own melodies. I did all this by ear. I would be on that piano day and night, driving my family crazy. Since age ten, I sang in the choir and in the youth group of my church, Coral Hill Baptist Church in Glasgow.

I made my commitment to Jesus Christ in a KOA[2] campground at a youth retreat. There was a speaker there from Dwight L. Moody Ministries. I was twelve years old, sitting in the back, flirting with the eighteen-year-old youth director I had a crush on. I was not paying attention to the message, but I remember hearing the speaker say he had the whole Bible memorized. I was impressed by that because, outside my bedroom door, we had a bookshelf of books from A to Z, and I was determined that I was going to learn all those books—so I started reading them from the beginning

---

1. DeFazio and Spencer, *Redeeming the Screens*, 82-84. "Used by permission of Wipf and Stock Publishers." www.wipfandstock.com.

2. Kampgrounds of America, Inc.

to the end. I had a thirst for knowledge. I started listening when the speaker said that he had memorized the Bible in its entirety. I recall finding myself at the foot of the altar, crying, not knowing what was happening to me, but my experience was so powerful that I looked back at my friends and thought: why am I here, and why are they back there? I recall that the camp leaders lit candles, and everybody who got saved walked with a candle to a cross in a field, then stood and sang as a part of the youth festivities. I do recall feeling alone at that moment as far as my friends went, but I also felt so full of peace, joy, and freedom, as well as a deep love for the Lord. I had a love relationship with Jesus starting in my heart. My friends could not understand what was happening to me. I did not want my parents to know what was happening. My dad was not a Christian, and I recall feeling set apart and different from everyone else because the experience was so powerful. The next day, I went out in the field and read my Bible, and the word came alive to me. I went to be alone in the field because I did not want my parents to see me.

Pastor Larry Doyle showed up at our house that afternoon. I remember my mom saying to me, "Can you come out here?" I was nervous about what had happened because none of my friends had come up. I thought: what is my mom going to think? A fear came over me that was trying to shut down my testimony before it had really begun, even my testimony to my own family. I did not know if my family had had this experience or not. My experience was so powerful and transformational that I did not understand it. My mom recalls that I prayed for a kitten of ours that had been run over by a car. My mom said, "Your kitten got killed," and I prayed for this kitten. To this day my mom still talks about this incident: Tiger the kitten got up and walked away like nothing had happened to him. My mom knew then that something was going on in my life for Tiger to be healed through my prayers. This realization is still within me now: under certain circumstances, fear still tries to keep my testimony from being revealed—because that testimony is empowered by the Holy Spirit. John, in Revelation 12:11, explains that we overcome by the "blood of the Lamb and by the word of their testimony." I want our readers to know that their own testimonies can be powerful.[3]

Worship is the call of God on my life. I have been on high profile worship teams: Billy Davis and Marilyn McCoo's *Soldiers for the Second*

---

3. DeFazio and Spencer, *Redeeming the Screens*, 84. "Used by permission of Wipf and Stock Publishers." www.wipfandstock.com.

Coming in Burbank, Dyan Cannon's *God's Party* at CBS Studios in Burbank, and Joanne Cash's Cowboy Church in Nashville. I currently worship with a great team at the Ojai Presbyterian Church in Ojai, CA.

I am participating in this dialogue on improvisation and street theater as Christian outreach because as a student at Liberty Bible College,[4] I sang and played guitar on the streets of Pensacola. A group of us from college (Rob, Lisa, Patty, Roger, and I) worshiped as a street ministry in downtown Pensacola in "the district." The historic district is a lot like New Orleans: it is a home to French Creole, Spanish Colonial, and British Arts, as well as nitty gritty bars and a night life of debauchery. Street performers abound in "the district." We brought the Holy Spirit to "the district," singing Christian worship hymns on its sidewalks. Passing tourists and transients alike recognized the words and melodies of traditional worship hymns we offered up to God's heavenly throne down in "the district" where drug trafficking and prostitution were common sights.

We also organized a Pensacola Beach ministry, drawing a crowd by building a campfire on the beach, singing and playing guitar. We sang some hymns, and some upbeat fun songs as well. People of all ages would come up for prayer after we performed. We prayed and ministered to everyone with words of encouragement from Scripture. It was a powerful experience as the music drew everyone to us.

I recall having a conversation with a Jewish guy one night. He knew the Old Testament by heart. Speaking with this Jewish young man made me realize that there was so much about the Jewish tradition in the Bible that I needed to learn. I knew from my own experience that Jesus does not judge us. He just gave and forgave us so that the truth could set us free to lead a life of peace and not a life of condemnation. I listened to him with love and no judgment, and the end result was him getting prayer and the loving touch of my Savior Jesus Christ—and all because I loved him to the truth. I never once pounded theology into him. It was the simple love of Jesus that flowed through me without judgment. That is what sets us all free—the love of Jesus. John 3:16 explains: "For God so loved the world He gave His only begotten son that we would have life and life eternally."

Since that time, I have acquired numerous professional credits as a singer and song writer. Accolades from the press and fans and colleagues are great. But I will always treasure the way that my worship on the streets

---

4. Liberty Bible College was founded by Ken Sumrall in 1964. In the early 1990s, Liberty Bible College in Pensacola closed the doors of its residential facility in Pensacola.

of Pensacola cut a path in the heavenly realm leading souls to Jesus. That is why I am encouraging performers to do outreach with their talents on the streets.

Resources

My music is available on my website, reverbnation.com/angelwithsoul. For a video of LeaAnn Pendergrass, host of *Uniting the Nations,* interviewing me, visit youtube.com/watch?v=_-c7KwkKCRo. If you would like to have me speak or sing at an event, or consult, please contact me by email at sheripedigo@gmail.com.

Afterword

William David Spencer

Berkeley Street Theatre performance in Sproul Plaza, University
of California at Berkeley, circa 1970

One sunny Mediterranean day, shimmering with that blue and white glow that distinguishes Greece and its islands, my wife and I were strolling along a street in Athens when we came upon a large crowd gathered in a public square. This was a time when sentiments by the Greek Orthodox Church were running anti-evangelical, intermittently dependent on the patriarch in power, and occasionally expressed against what was perceived as attempts to proselytize followers of the state church into dissenting splinter churches. In the center of the gathering was a street theater troupe. Though street preaching was currently a target for disapproval, it was also unlikely that all these diverse young people spoke Greek adeptly enough to get themselves detained by communicating their version of the gospel, complete with an altar call. But they had clearly figured out a way to circumvent the problems of language and legality, though their presentation was clear and uncompromising: they were performing the story of Jesus's passion, crucifixion, resurrection in mime.

As in Psalm 19:1-2, which tells us, "The heavens declare the glory of God; the skies proclaim the work of his hands. Day after day they pour forth speech; night after night they display knowledge. They have no speech; they use no words; no sound is heard from them, yet their voice goes out into all the earth, their words to the ends of the world" (TNIV), the message of this troupe was riveting the crowd—despite the fact there was no audible speech and no words and no voices.

Nothing was being conveyed that would offend the state church or compromise any historically orthodox dissenting one. Simply being depicted was the pure message of Jesus's great advent, sacrifice, and resurrection triumph to which all true Christians assent.

As I watched these young performers, the present faded for me and I sensed again the excitement in street theater, music festivals, and coffee house performances that communicated the serious message of the gospel decades in the past.

Art Was a Central Means of Communicating True Good News in the Jesus Movement

In its day, the Berkeley Street Theatre was just such a powerful drama ministry, both radical in style, yet centrist in proclaiming God's love through Jesus, despite, or perhaps because of, its countercultural context and trappings. The Christian World Liberation Front of the United States' west coast was a beacon of light in art, as this book reflects. Dr. David Gill, with whom I have had the blessing to serve as a colleague at Gordon-Conwell Theological Seminary, is right on target when he observed in the opening sentence of his foreword that "the 'Christian World Liberation Front' . . . was one of the liveliest, boldest, and most creative movements on the planet." The same could easily be said about the entire Jesus Movement, fueled as it was by a true moving of the Holy Spirit, evident in its concern for sound, historically orthodox theology, its opposition to war and violence, marijuana, heroin, and other illegal drugs, sexual immorality, and rampant materialism, all propelled by a creative explosion in art, music, theater, dance, creative worship.

When some today see the old photos of exuberant fountain baptisms and long-haired, t-shirted Jesus Freaks serving food to cultural refugees washed up upon the uncertain shores of city parks and squares, they may imagine that the profound message of Jesus's great work on behalf of humanity was cheapened and truncated in the hoopla of buttons and banners and slogans. But a document from that day tells a different story.

In a newsletter sent out by the "Street Theatre" itself, circa late 1974-'75, present editor, Jeanne DeFazio, gives a thoughtful report on "Fall 1974 . . . my first season in the Berkeley Street Theatre." Explaining the plays the troupe was performing, she notes: "Collage uses banal commercial advertisements to expose inculcated false social values. These advertisements and related elements of Christian truth are juxtaposed." "The Great Divorce is an adaptation of C.S. Lewis' fantasy. There is an emphasis, in this play, on the individual's choice to accept or to reject God's love. In a striking and beautiful way, this play shows the joy of those who accept grace and the unhappiness of those who reject it." "In Registration, there is a contrast shown between the interest of bureaucracies in all of us, and God's loving interest in each of us. One of the play's characters delivers an exhortation from the prophets." As she reflected on her experience, she observed: "The visual nature of these themes has influenced me. When I perform in Collage, Registration, or The Great Divorce, my professional sense of responsibility to my character and the play is strong. But the urgency of the play's theme is what really motivates me. It gives me a stronger sense of purpose in my life and in my work. You tell people who aren't Christian that the members of your theatre group are Christian and they say, 'Oh . . . , do you do Christmas pageants?'...We want people to walk away from these shows feeling that they have been given a picture of reality, the universe as it is and how God intended it to be."

This, of course, was Jesus's goal in his ministry. The power of performance is one that Jesus himself knew well. I believe he regularly employed it, perhaps acting out his one person presentations that we call parables. Some of these appear to be theatrical monologues, since they have characters with speaking parts. For example, how did he deliver the rich man's inner dialogue? Was it with a self-satisfied sneer? "I will do this: I will pull down my barns and build larger ones, and there I will store all my grain and my goods. And I will say to my soul, 'Soul, you have ample goods laid up for many years; relax, eat, drink, be merry!'" And how did he deliver God's angry reply, "You fool! This very night your life is being demanded of you. And the things you have prepared, whose will they be?" (Luke 12:18-20). Were these powerful speeches really done in a monotone? Or what about the vineyard owner snapping at his gardener, "See here! For three years I have come looking for fruit on this fig tree and still I find none! Cut it down! Why should it be wasting the soil?" Can't you hear Jesus shouting that—and then switching to the pleading of the gardener, "Sir, let it alone for one more year, until I dig around it and put manure on it. If it bears fruit next year, well and good; but, if not, you can cut it down" (Luke 13:7-9). And how did he render the heartrending plea of the miscreant son, throwing himself at last on his parent's mercy, "Father, I have sinned against heaven and before you; I am no longer worthy to be called your son . . . " And what did Jesus do with the father's poignant reply, "Quickly! Bring out a robe! The best one! And put it on him; put a ring on his finger and sandals on his feet. And get the fatted calf and kill it! And let us eat and celebrate! For this son of mine was dead and is alive again; he was lost and is found!" (Luke 15: 21-24). Do we think Jesus delivered it like he was reading off a caravan schedule? Did the master story teller, who was God-Among-Us in human incarnation, rivet his audiences any less than did the street theater troupe in Athens with their silent recounting of Jesus's own story or the Berkeley Street Theatre with their innovative plays depicting his message? Not likely! The story of Jesus is the Great Drama of loss and redemption. And it is what gives drama its power. When stories being enacted celebrate it with skill and excellence, theater flexes its muscles. And this is what happened in Berkeley, California in one of those exciting times when the Holy Spirit was racing through the United States and Canada and street theater "pitched its own tent" out among the people, as the original Greek wording of John 1:1

tells us Jesus did—and once again the Great Drama was celebrated before a new generation.

So, as I was working through the manuscript of what would become this book, gathering up data for this conclusion, and, frankly, simply enjoying reading about the thrill that pulsed in the Jesus Movement, I found myself wondering what role the Berkeley Street Theatre actually played in the larger movement itself. Recorded in this book, we have precious memories from the dramatic artists themselves, but was there a larger impact of their work? And how did their ministry fit in with the theological content and the art forms most promoted in the larger movement? Where would I search for an answer to such a question? As a participant myself in the east coast version of the Jesus Movement, I had collected a variety of original Jesus Movement material from 1969-1976 (over forty years ago at this writing). These were primary source documents, printed voices of the time in an explosion of Jesus newspapers that suddenly appeared spontaneously across the United States. I wondered if the thoughtful Berkeley Street Theatre was going to prove to be an anomaly. Was the Jesus Movement itself only intelligent in pockets and was much of it really just hoopla, as some may wonder? As I read paper after paper, I heard their voices tell a very different story. I discovered that, what Christian World Liberation Front did in microcosm, the Jesus Movement did in macrocosm: it was concerned with serious theology, promoted by its art, just as the serious message of CWLF was disseminated artistically by the Berkeley Street Theatre. But, just as there is no short-cut to excellence, a simple "take-it-from-me" does not really empower readers to draw their own conclusions. I realized the best way to trace the story of the context of Berkeley Street Theatre and its part in the larger movement, even given the restraints of a book, was to present examples of each of the papers I had gathered, discuss the theological interests reflected in them, the social concerns treated by them, and the art forms both being promoted in them and being used by them to convey the good news of Jesus. The appropriate place to start, of course, was with the Jesus newspaper of Berkeley Street Theatre's own "parent" organization: The Christian World Liberation Front's *Right On.*

A multi-fold thrust of historically orthodox theology and activist evangelistic and social outreach, with a heavy emphasis on creative art as a conduit, all to promote the building of God's reign by the lifting up of Jesus Christ can be seen in CWLF's free paper *Right On* (ancestor of today's *Radix*). Guided by the adept and indefatigable hand of Sharon Gallagher, with a staff including Ginny Hearn, present authors David Gill and (the then) Arnie Bernstein, cult expert Brooks Alexander, among several others, *Right On* included its own book editor, Jack Buckley, as well as a rock editor, Paul Baker, and a photographer Steve Sparks, partnered with a slew of art directors like Joe Peck, Shelly Korotkin, Nancy Bishop, et. al, to blend pop art, evangelical theology, and social concern in an eye-catching mix. Two examples demonstrate the sweep of its vision. The September 1971 issue opens with an outstanding cover of a rugged cross over an ancient astrology chart under a beautiful calligraphic of the paper's name: *Right On*. The issue features the first in a carefully written dissection of astrology by Jerry Excel, beginning with an engaging opening sentence from Africa, "Where the sky is, God is too," as this author contrasts the "God of the Hebrews . . . a 'jealous' God, who would not tolerate it if his people worshipped the other spirits in the universe, the 'elemental spirits of the world' as Paul calls them."[1] Then CWLF founder Jack Sparks delivers the bad news on trying to achieve "perfectibility" without God (attacking Charles Reich's bestseller, *The Greening of America*, as "superficial and stylized"), alongside book reviews of Alvin Toffler's *Future Shock*, Francis Schaeffer's *The Church Before the Watching World*, Lambert Dolphin's *The Church Is Alive*, and J. Herbert Gilmore's *When Love Prevails*, while the good news of Jesus is shared in an article, "Varieties of Pleasurable Experience," contrasting temporal and eternal pleasure, an interview with Arnie Bernstein on Jews for Jesus, and a back page support of Billy Graham's Oakland crusade with an observation that the attacking *Berkeley Barb*'s dismissal of the event as "'opium of the lasses' . . . represents new heights in male chauvinism and derogation of women."[2] Flash forward from the early days to the end of David Gill's timeline for the life of the first phase of CWLF, the December 1975-January 1976, vol. 7, no. 5 issue of *Right On*, and we find featured a central article by John Stott on "The Authentic Jesus"; six original sonnets by Walter Hearn; an extended book review article on the work of Christian poets Luci Shaw, John Leax, H. Houtman out of Toronto, Margaret Avison, Kathleen Spey-

---

1. Excel, "Astrology: The Sky Gods," 3.

2. Androcles, "Graham Crusade Freak-Out," 8. Not afraid to take on its critics, *Right On* also spoke up in its own defense, objecting to a reductionist article in the politically-oriented *Ramparts*, which accused "Jesus Freaks" of promulgating "thundering fear of hell and a candy-sweet promise of heaven." Eloquently setting the record straight, *Right On's* "Open Letter" referenced in its short half column defense Sartre's play *Dirty Hands*, the banning of good literature in the Soviet Union, and God's coming judgment on America.

ers, Heather Marsman, Steve Turner out of England, Calvin Miller's '70s classic, *The Singer,* along with the work of other Christian poets; a young David Gill's own exposition on what it takes to be a "Radical Christian"; a composite piece by readers promoting global "incarnational art" for Christmas from India, Guatemala, Jerusalem, Jordan, Appalachia as opposed to American commercializing of the holiday, wherein "our individual overconsumption is adding to the monumental economic problems in our world. The mind-blowing inequities of consumer buying power across the globe are little helped by American Christians who have adopted the 'more, bigger, and better,' cultural buying norm. In addition, super-concern about things and possessions is antithetical to the kind of priorities Jesus outlined (see Matthew 6: 19-33)." These pieces are followed by a back page summary of global news, focusing on "Torture in Brazil," "Baptism in China," and an analysis of "Zionism and the U.N." Not exactly "Jesus-Lite," was it?

In these two examples of early and later *Right On* issues, evangelical orthodox writings and actions of the time were examined and the artistic vehicle conveying the message was superior graphics (a rugged cross superimposed over an ancient astrology chart to advertise its lead article, "Astrology: The Sky Gods" on the early issue and a stained glass type depiction of "The Authentic Jesus" to promote the John Stott piece on the later one). Such mind-stimulating graphics were placed skillfully throughout the two issues and comprised the central art form in play (while poetry was also featured in the later issue).

Another California offering, a Hollywood-based, serious, heavy dutycontent Jesus paper relying more on the art-form of photographs with a mix of original graphics mixed with clip art and two poems in an example from volume 1, no. 10, of *The Alternative,* cost a dime and featured provocative interviews with California Christian movers like Dr. Donald Williams, "a Presbyterian Youth Minister at the resonate Center of a Nationwide Jesus Revolution. Passionate, earnest, informed—this Man's Jesus Makes Sense, and the Kids seem to know it"; a dialogue between a student and "the late James Morgan, Professor of Ethics"; original articles like author Lambert Dolphin's "Taking the Incarnation Seriously" (introduced with a reproduction of Ron Cobb's sardonic *Los Angeles Free Press* cartoon, "Will the real Jesus please ascend," with 3 Jesuses (Protestant, Historic, Catholic) as quiz show contestants; a thoughtful article on "Pornography & Personhood," a positive critique of Charles Reich's *The Greening of America* by associate editor Bill Goff, a plea for humility in evangelism, conveyed by a self-critical cartoon and poem against the self-aggrandizing Christian proselytizers (with a searing last stanza: "And He might reply/to those with pride:/'I never knew you, Soul-Winner!"), and selected, reprinted pieces from C.S. Lewis, an extended review of Francis Schaeffer's *The Church at the End of the 20ᵗʰ Century* by philosopher Richard Russell of Illinois's Trinity Christian College from *Vanguard*, a Bill Banowsky, "Alternative to Boredom," excerpted from the book *It's a Playboy World* and more in this eight page Jesus tabloid, well worth the 10 cents investment.[3]

Steeped in graphics, photos, and poetry, and reporting "World Wide Circulation 1 million,"[4] Jesus People's *Hollywood Free Paper*, edited by Duane Pederson, centered on first person profiles. Some of these were with celebrities promoting Jesus, for example, a picture of musician Judy Collins with an article on John Newton, "Ex-Slave Trader Writes #1 Hit," about the release of her version of "Amazing Grace," or an interview with actor James Fox on his conversion to Jesus.[5] So it showed an interest in music and cinema. But mostly it profiled young converts rescued from such pits as drug addiction to show Jesus's ability to rescue addicts of drug use (e.g., "Veteran Of Over 200 Trips says: 'I had to do something always because I didn't want to be bored . . . ,'" being the account of a hyperactive, attention deficit disordered Baptist youth whose drug use left him "almost dead, physically and mentally," until, desperate, "I started reading the Bible . . . I wanted to work and have a good healthy life . . . I began going to Bible studies, and things that I had known before in Sunday School became really relevant, and things that I read in the Bible became so important to me that I wanted to tell everybody about them."[6]). The same issue included "An Open Letter to Timothy Leary," amidst a vast multi-page, fine print set of announcements from all over the United States, Alaska to Texas and even

3. Edited by Rich Lang and five other associate editors contributing pieces to the issue, *The Alternative* was based at 6035 Carlos Street, Hollywood, California. Internal data suggests a date c. 1971. Neither "Soul-Winner" nor the cartoons are credited, 7.

4. Vol. 4, issue 1.

5. Vol. 3, issue 21, 2, 5.

6. Mark Lindley, "Veteran of Over 200 Trips says 'I had to do something always because I didn't want to be bored . . .'" *Hollywood Free Paper*, vol. 3. issue 17, 3. 1971. As a sampling, see also in the same issue, Paul Johnson, "Acid is a Teddy Bear" (against LSD); 2, Kevin Klier, "Last Christmas I Felt Guilty Because It Was Christmas and I Had Nothing In My Heart," a first person profile against alcohol and drug addiction, ; Jerry Lingenfelter, "From Drugs to Jesus," and another sally against drugs in "Want to Know How to Receive Living Bread?" page 7 in vol. 3, issue 21; Paul Johnson's "Shooting Up Satan," using the drug motif for an article against involvement in the occult is in vol. 4, issue 1.

Canada, promoting Prayer Meetings, Bible Studies, Rap Sessions, Festivals, Fellowships (like InterVarsity and Youth for Christ), many musicians and bands, and even, in one issue, a heart-rending personal plea: "Amelia (Millie) Marie . . . Please contact your Father. He is heartbroken, and wants you to know you are not wanted by the law. REPEAT . . . YOU ARE NOT WANTED BY THE LAW."[7] Of course, each issue featured a different graphically designed explanation of the steps to find salvation in Jesus Christ. I wondered as I reread these bold testimonies, emphasized by eye-catching pop-art, how many denominations these days are weighing in against legalizing cannabis or recognizing it for what it is: an entry drug into addiction for today's youth?[8]

Also, farther up the west coast, first class photography propelled *Truth* out of Spokane, Washington, a national clearing house of activist "Street Christian" news that, in one exemplary issue, features a page 2 lead article on "Jesus' People" in Louisville, Kentucky, "Street Christians" drawn from Southern Illinois University Students, conversions in Grangeville, Idaho, hippies and churches united for revival in Minot, North Dakota, a report on a Jesus rock concert in Danville, Illinois featuring Bob Hartman, himself a former drug user, rescued by Jesus to become the principal guitarist and songwriter of Dove and later of Petra (whose eponymous album was released by Word in 1974, followed by many others). The concert was co-planned by a 19-year-old woman who, having been delivered from drug addiction, Buddhism, and witchcraft, "accepts the label Jesus Freak."[9] Features follow on San Francisco, North Alaska, and, of course, news about "Street Christian" evangelism in Spokane, in this case done by a former female impersonator and an ex-gay friend who share their love of Jesus so gently with those they encounter "in the downtown area of Spokane . . . known as the 'fruit-loop,'" that, rather than being greeted with argument,

---

7. Volume 3, issue 21, 7.

8. Pilgrim Church, our 30 year, by this time of writing, store front church ministry, has worked with numerous drug addicts over these years, partnering with Adult and Teen Challenge, His Mansions, The Salvation Army, and the secular Center for Addictive Behavior. Every single heroin addict with whom we have worked began with marijuana – every one. This is my fiftieth year of city ministry. That is the pattern I've observed.

9. JSNI, "'Christians' Closed to Jesus News," 4. Voice of Elijah, the publisher, was an "incorporated" ministry. The president and director was Carl A. Parks and the editor, Bruce Schlettert.

eyes fill with tears as they are told, "I'm happy for you." Four accompanying photographs show smiles and tears amidst irenic conversations.[10]

In all this celebration of unity, one standout lament tells a sad story of rejection at an evangelistic crusade in Louisville. When street Christians attempted to hand out copies of *Truth*, attenders snapped, "Why don't you go peddle your garbage somewhere else . . . ?" To the reply, "This isn't garbage, it's about Jesus," the retort was: "If you want to know about Jesus, go listen to Bob [presumably the evangelist], he'll tell you all about him." "Jesus Freak: 'I know about Jesus. That's why I'm here.' Comment: 'Yeah, sure.' Jesus Freak: 'Jesus loves you.' No comment."[11] *Truth* itself was very sensitive to prejudice and to its correction, relating a center story about a police detective whose encounter with a "Jesus Freak" resulted in "Prejudice Against Long-hairs Gone."[12] It also noticed something that none of the other issues of Jesus newspapers I have did. Obviously, observations drawn from a few dozen Jesus papers against the vast array that were issued can hardly be conclusive, but in the several dozen sampling I have, I've noticed that feature articles on Anglo-Americans predominate. This same issue of *Truth* that laments prejudice and applauds its discarding features an article on a young African-American male who "wanted to be an example to the black people" and so he embraced Jesus and "I'm learning as much as I can and telling everyone I see about Jesus." It also features an article, "The Salvation Army Looks at the 'Jesus Freaks,'" reprinted from *The War Cry*, May 29th, 1971. Artistically, the issue is driven by many well done examples of you-are-there photography of "Door to Door Jesus Freaks," as the final back cover article announces,[13] and the art form it most promotes is music.

The first issue of *The [Boulder, Colorado]) Fish* presented a Jesus newspaper with all the trimmings: cartoons, hard-hitting free verse poetry, a back page poster of James 3:13-4:10 with graphics of bombs and an anti-war spin, while inside featured its own intelligent article and even a reprint of a *His Magazine* piece by John Warwick Montgomery. This approach was maintained through issue 6, *The Fish* still presenting a large, four-page tabloid, cartoons, poems, its own critiques of humanism and reprints of articles by then popular evangelical scholars, backed with its interesting final full page graphic illustrations, and, peppered throughout, with many book

10. Ibid., 4-5.

11. Ibid., 2.

12. Ibid., 8.

13. Ibid., 16.

reviews (e.g., Helmut Thielicke's *Nihilism*, released by Shocken books). *The Fish*, with its arresting graphics and its popular, thought-provoking content was an accessible production, similar to other Jesus papers of its time. Issue 8 suddenly changed its format into a heavy duty, nearly pocket sized barrage of content, now calling itself, "a journal of commentary, both on specific events and on general trends of today." Though the cover still retains calligraphic letters for its name above a fish insignia with the word for a fish, "*ichthus*," in Greek, and four of this large paperback book-sized twenty-four-page issue are illustrated with cartoon stick-figures, it was now free of hippie jargon and all its former Jesus newspaper visuals, adding many more articles which cite and interact with numerous scholars and local speakers. For examples, in an article on "Futurism" it quotes "E.J. Mishan, Reader in Economics at the London School of Economics," critiques the New Morality view of one George Leonard, an attorney from Washington (presumably D.C.) in "Instead of Morals," and dissects a World Affairs Conference, from Friday, April 2, 1971, suggesting this is a publication by intelligent Christian college students, whose identities are only given as Bob and Pete[14] (and in previous issues Steve and Mike), who are available at the Christian Book Booth in the UMC Loggia, Boulder (which translates to the University Memorial Center at the main campus of the University of Colorado, Boulder). Maybe its change of appearance was simply due to two different editorial preferences. Issue number 9 that followed, however, became a middle ground: *The Fish* had found a middle size, still maintaining a political dimension with articles like "Peace and the Pentagon Papers," while counseling readers, in "Two Kinds of Peace," "Don't worry about warring nations and political forces. God can give life and peace regardless of circumstances. Jesus said, 'Peace I leave with you. I give you my own peace and my gift is nothing like the peace of this world.' (John 14:27)"[15] But now it had added a photograph of a baptism by two long-haired (one of these bearded and bandana-wearing) Jesus Freaks, yet still maintaining its academic mission by reprinting an article by Jacques Ellul along with its own original articles, "How To (and Not to) Be Controlled by God" (more academic) and "Are You Following the Real Jesus?" (more popular in style), along with four pages of hand-written Bible verses, "adapted from *The Cambridge Fish*," and with cartoons and graphics scattered throughout. In the span of one year, 1971, *The Fish* had mutated from Jesus newspaper

---

14. *The Boulder Fish*, 1. No masthead or other information is included.

15. Pete Kelly, "Two Kinds of Peace," 7.

to college student journal to a moderate presentation of both, suggesting the pressures pulling at its young editors, as they alternately responded to the culture, the counter-culture, their present academic setting, and, perhaps, their church past and what might become their ecclesiastic future in a more conventional presentation of the gospel. But the accommodations suggested that, even in a day when their hair would be clipped and they were in the work force, employing their college degree, they would bring their excitement in the Jesus Movement with them. If there is one example in the larger milieu that might illustrate the pressures on the Berkeley Street Theatre ministry, this might be it. Here we see the counter-cultural appeal, the interaction with the world's false values, the appeal to reason (here with articles, there with thought-provoking drama presentations), a flux of change that affected both the college paper and the street arts, and the lack of stability for any ministry that is so innovative and responsive, suggesting that the days are precious and numbered and its participants only temporary in any milieu.

Not confined to California or the West, the Jesus Movement excitement had broken out in the east as well. For example, *The Well-Street Journal*, "a bi-monthly paper edited and published by a group of Christian students at the University [of Virginia] . . . while hosting articles of varying content and literary genre," announces "the concern of the Journal is Jesus Christ." The students add this disclaimer: "The Street Journal is not connected with any organization." The four-page "Journal," while depending on clip art, is driven by poetry and parable which fill its pages from a variety of sources, such as Gregory of Nazianzus, Richard Wilbur, and its own original poem by Rick Gustafson. But it still contains a mix, reprinting a poem from fellow Jesus Newspaper *The Liberator*, an article called "Reflections on the Revolution," by Leighton Ford, an articulate and thoughtful associate evangelist with the Billy Graham crusades, and the issue promotes both the upcoming Campus Crusade's "Explo-'72" and a Leighton Ford visit in the Spring, along with folksinger John Fischer and "a team from Gordon Divinity School in Boston" (a predecessor of today's Gordon-Conwell Theological Seminary, with which the present writer of this conclusion, the present editor, and the writer of the foreword are all related).[16]

16. Advertising weekly events of a Sunday night program called "Action 71" (with rides provided from "Memorial gym parking lot (South End))", *The Well-Spring Journal* appears to be a 1971 publication of upcoming events in 1972, this group of University of Virginia students gave their contact information as 1521 ½ West Main St., Charlottesville, VA 22903.

Washington D. C. Jesus People's (*Jesus Christ Is*) *The Liberator*, which *The Well-Street Journal* quoted, began its volume 1, number 1 maiden issue with an eye-catching cartoon cover, presaging the nearly all cartoon illustrated sixteen-page tabloid to follow, announcing its lead article by William Willoughby, Staff writer of the *Washington Star*, chronicling the rise of the Jesus Movement. The paper includes other features and lists over 260 Jesus People and associated ministries in thirty-one states, the District of Columbia, and Canada, including such entries as the innovative Melodyland with a Drug Prevention Center; Teen Challenge (now Adult and Teen Challenge); shelters like Berkeley's House of Maranatha and House of Pergamos for girls, as well as a version of the House of Pergamos for boys; Doxa Unlimited, Inc., offering a "Chapel open 8:00 a.m.-10 p.m. every day, Crash, Job Referrals, a Rap"; a "24-hr Hot Line," a Phoenix ministry called Agape, offering a crash (place to sleep) every night; other ministries offering meetings every night; "Powerhouse U.S.A., a 'gospel night club'"; campus ministries from Baptist to Catholic (e.g., "Pentecostal Prayer Meeting" at "Catholic University"); a vast array of coffee houses in churches (e.g., North Carolina's Winter Park Baptist), high schools (e.g., 7:30 a.m. at the "Wrestling Room" of Lexington [Kentucky] High School), and tucked into all sorts of other places; church showings of the silent *King of Kings*; dozens of musicians, including Larry Norman, Petticoat Faith ("Gospel & Pop folk, soft rock, All girls entertainment"), of course, the Jesus People USA's own Resurrection Band, with a page 3 add for a free Sons of Thunder concert at Washington D.C.'s Christ Church near American University, suggesting music is the art form of choice; numerous Bible studies; and even ethnic oriented ministries like California's "Chinese for Christ" at 1000 The Alamo and Venice Bible Church's "The Only Korean Jesus People Church In Los Angeles," highlighting "Korean Hippies Welcome," and many, many more items, validating *The Liberator's* own slogan, "Wherever you are, you are not far from a Jesus Center."[17]

Chicago's Jesus People USA (JPUSA) was issuing one of the most sophisticated of all the papers, *Cornerstone*, with beautiful, often full-color graphics. For example, issue 33 (1976) features a fold out front page graphic, its usual careful exposure of a cult (this month on "The Great Pyramid Intrigue"), an Os Guinness *Dust of Death*-inspired article on the decline of twentieth century humanity that quotes Erich Fromm, Allen Ginsburg, Herbert Marcuse; book reviews of Harold Lindsell's *Battle for*

17. Jesus People, *The Liberator*, 12-13.

the Bible and Francis Schaeffer's *How Should We Then Live?*, a Christian-themed hard-boiled detective graphic-novelish short story, *A Night at the Museum*, announcements for the Urbana missions conference, Billy Graham's upcoming crusade, ministries for "exploited women," warnings against "alcohol & brain deteriorization," alerts on countries that ban the Bible, support for "Quakers Stand Against Torture," and more global and domestic religious news. The issue is dedicated "in memoriam" to a former Latin Kings gang member, paralyzed in a bar fight, but finding Jesus and becoming a Christian and poet of praise for the last year of his life ("During the course of the funeral 12 people received Jesus in their hearts. Everyone knew George had died a child of the King of Kings, Jesus").[18]

Fielding their own bands, T-shirts, book publishing for several years (e.g., Mike Hertenstein's excellent *The Double Vision of Star Trek: Half-Humans, Evil Twins, and Science Fiction*), culminating each year in the Cornerstone Festival, JPUSA Chicago, with its panoply of in-house and outside Christian bands performing day and night, fine art exhibits, crafts shows, talks, and, of course, the same Mike Hertenstein's "Imaginarium," a high level set of sessions of film showings and critiques that have informed many Christian filmmakers, JPUSA remains today one of the greatest living legacies of the Jesus Movement.

Also in Chicago, bursting forth in the Fall of 1971 with its volume 1, number 1 fold-over back cover graphic of a black and white crucified Jesus wrapped in a red, white, and blue American flag, *The Post-American: Voice of the People's Christian Coalition* (the forerunner of today's *Sojourners*), under the guidance of editor Jim Wallis, asked a hefty 25 cents for the counter-cultural critiques of these rebels out of Deerfield, Illinois. Featured in the centerfold of the issue, the then Trinity Evangelical Divinity School Professor Clark Pinnock delivered a manifesto, "The Christian Revolution," with four theses, an explanation of "Revolutionary Values," and a "Modus Operandi" for applied action. The students take it from there. Artistically, outside of a front cover photograph of a protest march, the inside art is all popular graphics and cartoons (with eight raised fists, including the two famous Olympic ones), but otherwise appearing much like other Jesus papers, except this issue kicks off with a quotation from Albert Camus, announcing, "The World expects of Christians that they will raise their voices so loudly and clearly and so formulate their protest that not even the simplest man

18. "In Memoriam," 3.

can have the slightest doubt about what they are saying."[19] And protesting is what Jim Wallis tells us is the goal in his editor's note on page 15 of the issue: "In the People's Christian Coalition we affirm the orthodoxy of racial involvement . . . We have tried to show how the Gospel of Jesus Christ is indeed a liberating force which must be related to the turmoil of our times. Christian radicalism provides the vehicle and basis for change—for our own lives and our activism." Certainly Jim Wallis has delivered that radical Christian message right on through today, some forty-five years later. And back in 1971, *The Post-American* delivered as well. The issue culminated with "A Joint Treaty of Peace Between the People of the United States South Vietnam & North Vietnam" in the midst of this controversial bloody year of the so-called Vietnam "policing action," which all now recognize was a strangely denied yet certainly fought war. But before that radical ending, this first issue begins with Jim Wallis's own extended reflections on "Post-American Christianity," continues with Carlton Turner's redefining humanity on the ethic and model of Jesus, "A New Man," offers a critique of the Vietnam conflict and the United States' need for equitable housing, a poem on the misery of President Nixon, "Are There Tear Stains in the Oval Room?", a reminder that "If Christ Came Back Today," "He would certainly be 'crucified' in a 20th century way,"[20] reprints of an excerpt from Arthur Gish's *The New Left and Christian Radicalism* and Ann Stewart's "Silence" on racism from *The Other Side*. Bible quotations scatter throughout, sometimes graphically designed, along with a Frederick Douglass quotation, a forthright apology "In Defense of the Christian Faith" (graced by a cartoon judge with gavel pointing up the One-Way index finger sign), proclaiming, "We contend that the Christian faith – the religion promulgated by Jesus and continued by his disciples and the early apostles – is satisfying intellectually, ethically, and emotionally. It is the God-sent integration of head, hand and heart for ideologically fragmented man." Across from it is a Jim Moore silk-screened type poem poignantly re-envisioning Matthew 25, "i was hungry and you blamed it on the communists. i was hungry and you circled the moon . . . " - e.e. cummings as Christian radical (think cumming's own Luke 10:25-37-inspired poem "A Man Who Had Fallen Among Thieves" [1926]). Another reprint from *The Other Side*, John Alexander's critique of the "Madison Avenue Jesus" and even a bibliography of books from Stringfellow, Daniel Berrigan, H. Richard Niebuhr, Kierkegaard, Bon-

19. *The Post-American*, 1.

20. Loudon, "If Christ Came Back Today," 7. Jim Moore's poem is on page 13.

hoffer [sic], Stott, Bruce, Lewis, Montgomery, Gish, and even Malcolm X, make a meal of wide tastes along with nourishing foundationally applied Christian faith for one's mere 25 cents. By issue number 3, the price was dropped off page 1.

Free Love, the Jesus tabloid out of the several hundred-member Love Inn community outside Freeville, New York, is another sophisticated offering. Helmed by noted New York disc jockey Scott Ross and his wife, Nedra, formerly of the Ronettes, volume 1, number 1 (c. 1971) is an impressive twenty-four page archive of offerings: beginning with a four page, fifteen column interview with Noel "Paul" Stookey (of Peter, Paul, and Mary fame); articles by Ray and Marguerite Ruth Martin (published out of Finland) critiquing law, unjust law, and anarchy from their book *Quotations from Jesus and His Followers*; a seminary trained English teacher to present the gospel; a *New York Times* published feature on Love Inn; a three page profile of a former heroin pusher converted under the ministry of Nicky Cruz (of *The Cross and the Switchblade* fame) and Teen Challenge; an article critiquing "Reincarnation" by "M.G. (Pat) Robertson," "President, Christian Broadcasting Network, Portsmouth, Va.," and an impressive, globally sophisticated bibliography of over 150 books including works by C.S. Lewis, Walter R. Martin, Francis and Edith Schaeffer, Dietrich Bonhoeffer, Thomas A Kempis, Catherine Marshall, Watchman Nee, Hannah Whitall Smith, etc., and an equally impressive "compilation of record albums whose central theme is that of Jesus Christ" from Jimmy Durante to Edwin Hawkins, the Medical Mission Sisters to Cliff Richard, Larry Norman to Danny Taylor. The issue also includes a review of the "rock opera" *Truth of Truths* and Marvin Gaye's album *What's Going On*, as well as a listing of fifty-seven professional and nine college radio stations. Naturally, it includes an announcement for "The Scott Ross Show," according to *Billboard*, "a syndicated religious soft-sell program . . . produced by Larry Black . . . going great guns . . . now on the air in Bogota, Colombia, and Panama." "A Billboard award winner for Best Religious Program."[21] The art conduit was rock music, but included, in place of an editorial, was a very clever poem by Scott Ross himself, using song titles and familiar quotations of the time to point readers, captivated by its fresh approach, to Jesus.

---

21. *Free Love*, 23. Nedra Ross released a 1978 album on New Song Records, *Full Circle*, NS 005, produced by Scott Ross, and featuring instrumentation and background vocals by Phil and Bernadette Keaggy and many others.

Scott Ross, of course, was right on target in emphasizing music as the heart of the performance art form most evident in the reports of the Jesus Movement. No area in the United States centered on Jesus music more than did the East Coast (though little of it was recorded), and much of the most aggressive evangelistic use of music was centered in New Jersey. One exemplary church that became a center of Christian community and evangelistic outreach was the First Presbyterian Church of North Arlington. Its report of a Jesus Festival in January of 1972, released as a photograph filled four-page Jesus newspaper, *Good News of Jesus*, is a lesson in itself of what to do right in ministry. Driven by Director of Christian Education Rev. Jerry Davis, the church went all out to mobilize the surrounding churches as one unified community and it promoted all the fellow churches' ministries, identifying in which church each performing band was based and including a list of "Jesus Places" in the surrounding towns at two Baptist Churches, a Roman Catholic Church, the YMCA, and, particularly promoting, the new "Maranatha experience" out of New Milford, the beginning of this prominent Christian music ministry. The back cover of the church's Jesus newspaper featured students engrossed in other local Jesus newspapers with the caption, "People enjoy reading about what's happening in other places. The 'Mustard Seed' and "Maranatha' papers were very popular." And beneath the caption is an invitation in large print inviting all to "Send in The News!" adding, "You can help us make this paper more useful by sending in news of your group and what's happening where you are. News stories, announcements, listings of Bible studies, Coffeehouses, Fellowship meetings, special events, projects, whatever!" The church was not using the Festival to turn itself into a mega-church. It was using it to promote everything related to the new sudden interest in Jesus in all their great variety of expressions. So, at its festival, it featured a presentation, "Jesus and the Drug Thing," by Teen Challenge of nearby Paterson, which it described as an "anti-drug, pro-Jesus organization that grew out of David Wilkerson's work with the young gang members in New York City, as described in the best-selling book, 'The Cross and the Switchblade.' It also scheduled a number of other sessions, including one on "Jesus and Prayer" led by the "President of the newly formed Full Gospel Businessmans (sic) Association, Ramapo Chapter," adding the speaker "is a frequent guest of the 'Mustard Seed' Coffeehouse at Ramsay." Another session went to a group of priests, led by "Father Bill O'Brian," Roman Catholic Student Chaplain at Fairleigh-Dickerson [Dickinson] University in Rutherford, who, with Father Jack Sutton, "helped provide answers at an exciting discussion focusing on 'Catholics and the Jesus Experience.'" Other sessions included "a Director of HiBA Clubs" (High School Born Againers), "The Jesus Movement and What it Means to the Churches," a showing of 'The Gift,' a United Presbyterian produced film that presents the Gospel through an unusual style of animation," which "attracted many viewers," and a promotional "special showing" in the church's "audio-visual room" of 'The Maranatha Story,' a film-strip of the New Milford Experience," "produced by the church and photographed by Look magazine staffers."[22] Here is a church that was a living lesson in promoting the Spirit of unity that marked the best of the Jesus Movement Revival. And what attracted the 1200 young to this event was a huge roster of bands from all these churches and coffeehouses and ministries, highlighted by Rock Garden, the area's most prominent professional Christian band, along with Water into Wine, an aggressive evangelistic band out of Nyack, New York, and, of course, the Maranatha Band from New Milford. But I note in all this variety of artistic events no listing was made for any dramatic troupe performing. Had there been one with reach, I am certain it would have been invited to this eclectic event.

By the time I had listened to these many voices of the Jesus Movement, my question had begun to refocus. I began to ask: besides the Berkeley Street Theatre, were there any other Christian guerrilla theater or street theater troupes in prominence—or even in action? And, if not, why not?

On April 10 of that same year, 1972, Maranatha itself presented "Jesus Joy" at New York's Carnegie Hall, with Rock Garden, Danny Taylor, Andrae Crouch and the Disciples, and Lillian Parker, a watershed moment in East Coast, Jesus Movement History. In its Easter issue of *Good News of Jesus,* the First Presbyterian Church of North Arlington promoted that event with a full page announcement and a feature headlining article on "The Maranatha Story" in its Easter 1972 issue. Alongside profiling the New Milford church, its music ministry, its New Milford Coffeehouse, its pastor, Rev. Paul Moore, it also used its pages to promote Billy Graham's book on *The Jesus Generation,* various campus ministries, Campus Crusade's Explo '72 NJ contact, an Evangelical Free Church in West Orange, and only publicized its own ministry, Koinonia, by printing appreciation letters from participants, interviewing a family in the ministry, and reporting on a Koinonia Retreat. The rest of the space went to an article culled from *Christianity Today* about the Jesus Movement on college campuses, which featured a

---

22. Tonner, "1200 Celebrate at Festival," 4.1-2.

graphic of covers of other Jesus newspapers: *Right On, Truth, Hollywood Free Paper, Agape, Jesus Loves You*. Such self-less deference to other ministries is a reminder of something often lost in this push-yourself-forward-and-milk-each-activity-so-it-can-go-viral age.

As a twenty-four-year-old seminary senior, I and my soon wife-to-be, Aída Besançon, attended that memorable Carnegie Hall event. We ourselves had been deeply involved in the Jesus Movement in several versions of our own evangelistic folk-rock band, begun in 1966, before there was a Jesus Movement in our area and running right into the beginning of that year, 1972, when I and eventually Aída became college chaplains. Our band had played Jesus festivals (one in Bethlehem, PA on the same bill as Water into Wine, another in Cranford with Turley Richards), as well as coffee houses (when these got going), colleges, and churches throughout the New York, New Jersey, Pennsylvania area. In 1969, the band, called the Spheres, won a slot on WABC's Big Break with iconic disc jockey Bruce Morrow (then known as "Cousin Brucie"), a very welcoming and kind man in my experience, who encouraged new bands with gracious enthusiasm, and we had the opportunity to play that day before headliner Steppenwolf, having about 3 ½ minutes of temporal prominence in the *Courier News*, our regional newspaper, before that earlier acoustic folk version of our band suffered a fatal case of college graduation and we regrouped as a folk-rock band with electric guitars, drums, and percussion. On all our travels, we saw no Christian guerrilla theater performances.

Who would suspect the New York Bible Society International (NYBS) of publishing a "Jesus Paper," but that's exactly what *Great News* was, a 1969 "Eternal Edition" of the entire NIV Gospel of John in eight newspaper-sized pages, with pop art, photos, beautiful graphics, and even a One Way sign and an altar call at the end for readers to "admit you've blown it, like everyone else. Like, your life's been one big ego trip filled with rotten rip off things. Get it into your head that God thru Jesus loves you no matter how wasted you are. This is no plastic rap!"[23] It certainly wasn't. It went right along with their denim-covered Bible. No question the NYBS could rock with the times. Their vehicle was pop art of a high caliber.

Also out of New York was a Jesus paper called *Credence* and in its second issue it did something none of these other Jesus newspapers I reviewed had done. It had the usual creative graphics, and an advertisement for Maranatha's upcoming "Jesus Joy," placing this undated West 57th Street-based

23. New York Bible Society International, *Great News*, 8.

publication in late 1971 or early 1972. It had its own thoughtful articles, an extended critique of Stanley Kubrick's film *A Clockwork Orange* that went far beyond a simple movie review as its lead article, a critique of humanity, two examinations of the self (one beginning with a quotation from Dostoevsky's *Notes from the Underground*), a firsthand account by a Messianic Jew and a profile of a Staten Island coffeehouse, the "House of Ichthus." It also included advertisements—one for a jeweler, which is unusual—along with Christian bookstores and the American Bible Society, several short book reviews, including one, under the title "Exposes Occultism," reviewing McCandlish Phillips' *The Bible, the Supernatural, and the Jews*, complete with a Wesley Pippert endorsement from *The Alliance Review*, a short page of announcements of churches, including a Chinese Evangelical Mission, more listings of coffeehouses and a number of college fellowships, and in the centerfold a beautiful drawing of Jesus. In all this it maintained its own integrity as a Jesus paper, but it did one thing that we will notice none of the others reviewed did. Up until this point, the performance arts mentioned have been largely limited to musicians, single or in bands, but no other performance arts did we see featured or even listed until we come across an interview by 123 West 57th Street Calvary Baptist Church's Minister of Students Dennis Miller, who interviews Gregg Mitchell, a Julliard dance student under the title, "A Time to Dance." In this sensitive and perceptive discussion, Gregg tells his theology of dance, "a beautiful gift given by the Lord to express feelings and ideas with a total means of expression – the entire body. Dance is a perfect outlet for me to glorify and praise the Lord." Having "loved sports and been a hyper and physical person" he was guided by his mother into dance when he was ten-years of age. Now, as a professional, he is confronted with "a trial and a challenge to rise above the filth and nonsense." Required to "improvise a wild beast in a fit of rage against another animal[,] the Lord talked to my heart, and I knew He didn't want me to dance that along with a lot of profanity in dialogue and overt sexual groping in the choreography. He compelled me to leave the company." He has had to navigate regular advances by homosexual dancers and reject similar parts he will not play, but, at the same time, he has found many positive parts, and, under the influence of a tape his father gave him of Tom Skinner preaching on the church as "a huddle" wherein strategy is set to go into the streets, he has moved forward, encouraging other Christians: "My great concern is to see more entertainers wholly give themselves to God through Jesus Christ so that their talents will be used to glorify Him. Happily, the Kingdom of God is growing among artists and entertainers at Julliard and other places like it. There are growing corps of committed Christians. Praise the Lord!"[24] This "into the marketplace" commitment of a young dancer is a blessing to read and his total commitment to performance art and to serving the Lord Jesus Christ parallels that of the Berkeley Street Theatre.

This brings us to our final example, one of the most sophisticated and clever of the Jesus papers, *Ichthus*, out of Cherry Hill, New Jersey. Here we see announcements for "Ralph Carmichael's 'folk musical' NATURAL HIGH" at the Music Pier in Ocean City, NJ (September 8, 1971 issue) and the "Rock Musical," THE JOY EXPLOSION (Dec. 1971, vol. 1, no. 11), both fledgling examples of Christian musical theater. With my youthful ability to acquire Jesus newspapers sadly limited by coin and access (no money for subscriptions), these were the first announcements of their kind I can note in all the state by state summaries in the dozens of issues of Jesus newspapers I managed to gather at the time. I remember viewing several of these types of musicals, often presented by large groups of church youth, [25] as the one advertised from the First Baptist Church of Montclair, NJ, on December 5, 1971. *Ichthus* noticed and promoted such events in a detailed two-page newspaper sized spread of "Jesus Happenings," covering the east coast states of New Jersey, Pennsylvania, New York, Delaware, and Maryland.

Helmed by Editor Bob Patterson with a staff that included an accountant, distributor, mailer, subscription and bulk orders staff, circulation assistant, art editors (including Bruce McDaniel, bass player of our Spheres Jesus band and today's Circle of Friends, as well as author of his memoirs *Walk through the Valley: The Spiritual Journey of a Vietnam War Medic* and the science fiction novelette *Walk Together Earth Mother Children*), a typist, two book sales staff, and contributing writers, with editorial and business offices at one location and circulation and distribution at another, *Ichthus* was a one-stop shopping center for all Jesus Movement news. It fielded its own cutting edge articles like "God Uses Women," in the dawn of the then current revitalization of the evangelical women's movement, observing, "Jesus Christ has been accused of being a male chauvinist. So has Paul. Yet

24. Miller, "A Time to Dance," 4.

25. One ensemble piece visiting our all men's college campus appeared to be comprised of a large group of senior high schoolers who performed in a semi-circle across from the campus bookstore when I was a college senior. Enthralled, the freshman and sophomores were all mesmerized every time the girls suddenly turned their backs to them in the choreography, in order to whip around and sing, "Here's Life!"

such accusations have no justification. If you examine the Bible, you see that women are given much space." After praising many biblical women, the article centers in on "Priscilla, a woman about whom every woman should think." Observing "undoubtedly Priscilla studied and learned from Paul. Hearing Paul preach and teach daily must have been like a woman to-day hearing Billy Graham or John Stott or Francis Schaeffer every day," the article neatly promotes the leadership of Christian women by contextual-izing its message in its time. Pointing out Priscilla's courage to use her gifts, "in a period of time when women were not encouraged to use their heads, Priscilla was not afraid to use hers." Therefore, "Paul could trust Priscilla. He put her in charge at Corinth and then at Ephesus. He knew he could leave her and she would persevere in the faith . . . . leading without offend-ing or displaying herself." So, "the church in Rome was named for Priscilla, not Aquilla (sic). Despite her superior ability, she worked with Aquilla in real harmony, showing her ability to handle human relationships. She un-derstood him, accepted him and probably even led him without making him feel inferior. More evidence of her ability to lead is seen in her en-counter with Apollos. She straightened him out but she did not offend him or put him down." As a result, "Priscilla set a real example for all women . . . especially for those in positions of leaders or teachers." The article is unsigned, but the masthead notes that Norma Patterson is a contributing writer, so either she or Bob Patterson, or both composed this fore-thinking piece from *Icthus's* May 1972 issue.[26] The cry to liberate the use of women's gifts (and give credit for service where credit is due) of today's egalitarian evangelical movement represented by such organizations as Christians for Biblical Equality and such publications as those from the present House of Prisca and Aquila Series of Wipf and Stock, publisher of this book, were already resonating in the Jesus Movement, as we see here. In 1974, Aída Besançon Spencer would publish in the journal of the Evangelical Theolog-ical Society her seminal article "Eve at Ephesus" (predecessor to her classic work on women in ministry, *Beyond the Curse*), which she then delivered in April of 1975 to an astonished crowd of students and faculty at Pennsylva-nia's Westminster Theological Seminary.[27] In 1977, Don Williams (featured

26. Bob and Norma Patterson, "God Uses Women," 4.

27. Milling in the crowd during the break, anonymous because of my male sex and my equivalent age, I heard students buzzing about the presentation and greeting new arrivals with exclamations, "Hey, you just missed a great talk!" and "Ow! You just missed *the* talk!" For more of my reflections on that memorable day, please see my "Equaling Eden: A Practical Male Afterword" in my wife's book, *Beyond the Curse*, now out with

above in *The Alternative*) would publish *The Apostle Paul and Women in the Church* with Regal books, CWLF's the Hearns would emerge as evangelical egalitarian leaders, and on and on.

Art-wise, *Ichthus* depended on original and reprinted art, very cleverly chosen (like the Jesus Christ Wanted Poster, a Jesus Wants You! Announcement, taking off on the Uncle Sam one, etc.), produced its own articles as well as reprinted selected ones from such fellow papers as *Right On, The (Boulder, CO) Fish, The Hollywood Free Paper*, and many others, and, as we noted earlier, promoted whatever Jesus events or concerts it could find, including folk and rock musical performances. Had there been a Jesus performing troupe like Berkeley Street Theatre (BST) on the east coast it would have doubtlessly promoted that as well.

CWLF'S Berkeley Street Theatre Emerged Out of this Ferment, as its Founders and Participants in CWLF's Shared These Commitments.

Now, what have we learned from this detailed survey, digging into the national context of BST by listening to desultory examples of the printed voice of the Jesus Movement in which BST was formed? The Jesus Movement was serious about theology and intensely active in ministry. It was excited about liberation in Jesus, convinced that surrendering to Christ was the only true solution for human and societal problems. It had no illusions about the world's answers, eschewed its materialism, and opposed its solutions—narcotic, hedonistic, mercantile, and martial. It was contextual to the late 1960s-1970s, often dropped out, tuned in, and turned on—but to the Holy Spirit. In between its many book reviews, provocative articles, and lists and reviews of Jesus Happenings, it was pop and graphic art expressed, reviewing literature, creating poetry, featuring photography, and, particularly, being music driven. It established coffee houses and festivals that lent themselves space-wise to single performers or small bands. Craft and Fine Art were available, along with the posters, buttons, banners, T-shirts, many of these on sale in Christian bookstores. But performance art, like theater, was in its infancy, as a kind of new theater, as opposed to church pageants, the heirs of the medieval mystery plays. Guerilla theater lent itself to the movement, especially with such fervor in the air. But Christian-oriented

---

Baker Academic.

theater, dance, mime, and performance art were all in their developmental stage. Above all, its proponents across the sweep of the movement were steeped in the Bible, as the repository of the words of personal and societal life and wellbeing. And a lasting, stand-out impression is how the scholars worked together with the young people, contributing articles, speaking at college campuses, their publishers sending in their books for review.[28] Also astonishing was how much cooperation I found between the churches and the movement. Many churches sponsored coffee houses (like the Agape Coffeehouse we ran in the First Presbyterian Church of Dunellen, NJ, in cooperation with the Rev. Allen Ruscito, Andrew Blackwood III, and Elder Ned Holtzman, all enthusiastically supported for its three years' duration (1969-72) by the church eldership.

This is the matrix in which Berkeley Street Theatre became a developing experiment in communicating the gospel in an artful yet visceral manner. It was composed of intelligent, well-read, well-educated Christians, who were themselves steeped in the Bible, reading and writing and ruminating on the issues of the day, creating productions that brought a Christian perspective to these issues in arresting dramas that they took to the streets, as one intentional wing of the decentralized, mass cooperative endeavor of networked individual ministries that these Jesus papers chronicle.

What Was the Legacy for the BST Participants?

As I listened to the voices in this book, each reflecting on his and her part in creating this innovative ministry, here is what I heard. Editor Jeanne DeFazio cited Exodus 23:20, God's promise to sojourning Israel as encouraging and comforting as she stepped into the ministry, convinced that God would send an angel before her and bring her to the place where god intended to use the gifts she had been given. When that place was revealed as drama in the streets, Revelation 12:11 was added to her vision: she found victory in her dramatic testimony to Jesus Christ, a victory she continues to find in her writing, editing, and teaching.

---

28. One story I heard recently is that the renowned evangelical scholar Norman Geisler, still teaching apologetics today, invested much time and his great expertise in helping JPUSA in its formative years to grasp securely on to historically orthodox bearings and its continuing affiliation with the Evangelical Free Church.

Director Gene Burkett, "searching for a meaningful Christianity," found it in the nuts and bolts of piecing together street performances that could reach a variety of people, as he chose plays to help others find the door out of hopelessness: Jesus Christ. Psalm 28:7 became essential to him as he found the Lord, strengthening, protecting, and guiding him, a commitment that he continued in business, his legal advocacy work, and his many ministries.

Charlie Lehman reports he was motivated by his recognition of the power of theater to be prophetic and evangelistic. Hosea 4:1, driving the action of the play *Registration*, revealed the impersonalizing oppression of bureaucracies, as it lamented the presence of faith, kindness, and knowledge of God in society. In that sense, he noted, "the guerilla actor, like the guerilla soldier," trades "technical aids" for "adaptability, mobility, financial and therefore ideological freedom from the audience," like the disciples Jesus sent out, taking nothing but their faith into the streets. Charlie continued serving those from the streets in his work at the L.A. Public Defender's Office.

Susan Dockery Andrews focused on God's mandates in Micah 6:8: "What does the Lord require of you? To act justly, to love mercy, and to walk humbly with your God." These are deep seated, foundational ways to conduct one's life, and she saw the task of theater as being, not simply about sharing words, but about holding up this model as a kind of pre-evangelism of how to and how not to act. She also recognized a challenge before all thinking artists. Christian Philosopher Simone Weil, who gave her life in her identification with the sufferers of the Holocaust during World War II, observed, "Nothing is so beautiful and wonderful, nothing is so continually fresh and surprising, so full of sweet and perpetual ecstasy, as the good. No desert is so dreary, monotonous, and boring as evil. This is the truth about authentic good and evil. With fictional good and evil it is the other way around. Fictional good is boring and flat, while fictional evil is varied and intriguing, attractive, profound, and full of charm."[29] Susan Dockery Andrews thinking deeply about her experience, notes, "during this time, I began to wonder why it was so easy to portray destruction and negativity, but much more difficult to portray the good, true, and sacred as many-faceted and full-bodied." She brought this reflective approach to her work in dance (with the kind of company our young dancer Gregg informed

---

29. Simone Weil, "Morality and Literature," 290.

Dennis Miller he was seeking to find in his *Credence* interview), in arts administration, and in teaching.

Father James (formerly Arnold) Bernstein likened himself to the blind man healed by Jesus, recounted in John 9:35-38. His mission was to the world-blinded audience, realizing, "all beauty comes from God and reflects His creative love, with or without the attachment of a message. On the other hand, all of creation – including beauty – serves to remind us of God. So beauty and art have both intrinsic value and the power to draw us to God." And draw the "accidental" audience to God is what he and Berkeley Street Theatre did. Even when the attenders were "anti-Christian," "the audience loved us in spite of our message because the skits were presented creatively with artistic excellence and respect for our audience." Today, as a long-time leader in Christian ecclesiastical orthodoxy nationally and internationally, he is a model of action/reflection ministry, in his writing and in his service to Christ.

No wonder the Jesus Movement, with powerful ministries like Berkeley Street Theatre, is considered among the most recent of the real U.S.A. revivals (not just the fire-insurance scares like the non-event 2000 end-of-the-world dud). Its participants recognized themselves as sojourners in a fallen land, searching for authentic Christianity, lamenting fallenness and its continual damage to an audience they loved and respected, struggling themselves to present the good above the evil in a way that celebrated the faith, the loving kindness, and the justice of God, which was the goal in all the voices we heard in the larger Jesus Movement, as it united in its search and rescue of those lost in drugs, promiscuity, materialism, war, and despair to show the watching world the better way.

The Legacy of Theater Ministry Continues

Berkeley Street Theatre began in 1972 and, after many vigorous performances, as with CWLF, it sent its own participants across the states and the world both to begin and to enrich other ministries. Yet, for all its energy and commitment, it received but one reference in Larry Eskridge's amazingly detailed *Christianity Today* award-winning "Book of the Year," *God's Forever Family: The Jesus People Movement in America*, and that was when the author was noting "primary sources from the Jesus People are filled with announcements, anecdotal asides, and passing references to the matrimonial links being forged among the movement's numbers": "The

Christian World Liberation Front announced an upcoming wedding in one of its 1974 fund-raising letters: 'Peggy Lee has been with us for two years and is responsible for filling literature orders,' the letter noted. 'In June, she will marry Gene Burkett,' who had 'come to us recently to be with the Street Theatre."[30] The blame for such neglect of this seminal ministry does not necessarily lie with author Eskridge. He reported what he found. That guerilla theater was a living part of the overall ministry is undeniable, but that it was basically unpublicized and undervalued is also probably true too.

Faring better in terms of longevity has been a sister organization, the Lamb's Players, incorporated the year before BST in 1971, after its own birth as a class drama project at Bethel College in St. Paul, Minnesota. Professor Steve Terrell with student Glen "Herbie" Hanson launched a production they named "'The Hound of Everyman,' a contemporary comedy that used the form and costumes of the medieval morality plays." The next year, 1972, they moved to southern California and began Lamb's Players' steady rise, developing, beside their Street Theatre, troupes in mime, puppetry, dance, and "a juggling and magic act." Their "Street Theatre" ceased in 1986 to focus on education to schools "to address critical student issues like drug abuse, bullying, and the power of literature and language." Today, Lamb's Players runs two theaters, hiring "more San Diego based actors than any other company," fielding a budget in excess of four million dollars, and attracting more than 100 thousand attenders to its performances each year.[31]

Other groups, however, appear to have passed into obscurity, unsung in their day and unremembered except by the few in ours. Why is that?

One reason street theater did not receive more than passing notice may be that the churches, who were an integral part of supporting and furthering the Jesus Movement, began investing more in the folk and rock musicals that were, in part, a response to the British "rock opera" *Jesus Christ Superstar* and the American "Musical Based Upon the Gospel According to St. Matthew" *Godspell*. By 1973, both live performances and the corresponding movies of these influential pieces were now being performed and shown everywhere (fueled as well by the huge impact of Franco Zeffirelli's beautiful film on the life of St. Francis, *Brother Sun, Sister Moon*, with its haunting theme sung by the popular folkie turned psychedelic songster Donovan).

---

30. Eskridge, *God's Forever Family*, 252.

31. See https://lambsplayer.org/history and https://tickets.lamb'splayers.org .

Two early responders were both giants in the world of Christian music. Ralph Carmichael, a pastor's son from Quincy, Illinois, but reared in North Dakota and then in Southern California was as eclectic in his musical tastes as in his travels. His musical prowess catapulted him into arranging for such renowned television shows as "I Love Lucy" and the "Roy Rogers and Dale Evans" show. He also worked with famous performers such as Bing Crosby, Rosemary Clooney, Nat King Cole, and Ella Fitzgerald, and scored hits like pianist Roger Williams's movie theme: "Born Free." For Billy Graham, he wrote and arranged the music for a number of films, most notably, *The Restless Ones*, whose theme song contained one of the best bass-drum intros in Christian popular music of any era.[32] Partnering up with Kurt Kaiser, out of Chicago, an American Conservatory of Music graduate (among other schools), who himself had been working with Texas-based Baylor University, and had since arranged and produced for his own set of famous singers, including Tennessee Ernie Ford, Ethel Waters, Burl Ives, and Kathleen Battle, they set about creating a number of well-received "Folk Musicals about God," like *Tell It Like It Is* (named for a response by George Harrison of the Beatles to reporters which went the '60s equivalent of today's "viral"); *NATURAL HIGH* (their own response to use of illegal drugs wherein "Christ is our NATURAL HIGH"[33]); *I'm Here, God's Here; Now We Can Start*. *Tell It Like It Is* and *NATURAL HIGH* were wisely released on a label Ralph Carmichael created, ensuring less potential hassle negotiating any prejudicially conservative attitudes that might impede these pieces progress if such reluctance existed elsewhere in the Christian music industry of the day.[34] Both of these young seasoned

32. Released as a 4 song 45 RPM on Grason BG-6515 SK4B-2818, and as well on *Johnny Crawford Sings Songs from The Restless Ones* on the Supreme label S-210.

33. Carmichael, liner notes for *NATURAL HIGH,* back cover.

34. Light was a courageous label, including in its releases the soundtrack of Cliff Richards' *Two a Penny*, which covered songs like the Isley Brothers "Twist and Shout," Paul Simon's "Red Rubber Ball," an American hit in 1966 for The Cyrkle, and other pop rock songs, a daring move for a basically Christian label. But eclectic and daring is what Ralph Carmichael has been all about, releasing lush Christian big band albums like *One Hundred and Two Strings* (volumes 1 and 2) on the Sacred label, and back on Light, the barnstormer redux *The Piano I Remember*, as well as his beautiful *Christmas Joys*, one of our family's staple Christmas chestnuts. And he added in Jack Coleman's *The Centurion: An Easter Cantata,* which Ralph Carmichael himself conducted, along with his *I Looked for Love: Ralph Carmichael's Contemporary Sound* and even the experimental *Ralph Carmichael Presents The Electric Symphony [The MOOG Synthesizer]*. What an interesting label! And today he continues with more recent offerings available on his website: http://ralphcarmichal.com. His prowess is shared with his family. He produced

veterans were prolific songwriters and Ralph's "He's Everything to Me" (aka "In the Stars His Handiwork I See") and Kurt's "Pass It On" (aka "It Only Takes a Spark") were both included by the courageous music editor Donald P. Hustad's on his enduring 1974 *Hymns of the Living Church*, published by Hope Publishing Company, the hymnal that we still use today in Pilgrim Church, Beverly, Massachusetts.

A spate of other Christian ensemble pieces also appeared like Otis Skillings's *Life* on Tempo Records in 1970. Ray Ruff's 1971 *Truth of Truths: A Contemporary Rock Opera*, a professionally done, high quality, rock-driven extravaganza, from creation to incarnation, starring Dick St. John of Dick and Deedee fame ("The Mountain's High," "Thou Shalt Not Steal," "Turn Around"), without Mary Sperling, the original Deedee, but, instead, with Dick's wife, Sandy, an accomplished singer herself who had stepped in to become the new "Deedee" after Mary "retired to marriage and family,"[35] and also starring Donnie Brooks (of the lovely "Mission Bell," "Up to My Ears in Tears," and "Hollywood Party" fame). Also renowned composer and arranger Jimmy Owens and his talented songwriter wife Carol Owens produced *Show Me* on Impact, featuring Jesus music star Randy Stonehill, Contemporary Christian Music pioneer Michael O'Martian, and popular CCM singer Jaime Owens. And even a two record set on ARCO-Artists' Records of composer R.K. Wells and director (with her husband, Rocky) Alice Adkins' *I Wonder: a musical drama*, backed on record by the Greenville, Ohio Senior High School Band and performed by the Agapé Players, a touring group of young actors "traveling nine months out of the year" and covering "almost the entire United States and several provinces of Canada each tour,"[36] appeared among many others.

Evangeline Carmichael's lovely eponymous album on Sacred and his daughter Carol had an EP of six songs in the late 1960s that, if there were any justice in the rock firmament, should have been smash hits. Ranging from the catchy pop piece, "Love Minus One," the folk rocker "Brownstone Castle on Bleaker Street," the Brazilian-tinged "You Are Gone," and the haunting "Memories," this rare EP is a treasure and should be released for '60s music buffs of which there are many. Kurt Kaiser himself is still active, also in his '80s. His own virtuoso talents displayed on his Word album *Pass It On* (WST-8562) are still going strong with a new album of Christmas carols "olde" and new on his website: http://www.kurtkaiser.com/ Both these composers and arrangers have won numerous awards, but they never lost the humility that comes from true ministers always reaching out to those who need Jesus. As Kurt Kaiser wrote on his liner notes for *NATURAL HIGH*, the music is "honest, true unrefined and, we feel, 'where it's at.'"

35. Everett, liner notes for *The Best of Dick and Deedee*, 6.

36. Liner notes for The Agapé Players, *I Wonder: a musical drama* ARCO 710618,

Church-based dramatic and musical ministry began to thrive and left its own legacy as well as its impact as it branched out in various innovative directions that can be seen in the work of several other authors in the present book. For example, the stalwart Joanne Petronella revived the spirit of the old medieval mystery plays and continued long-term, among her many ministries, her "Good Friday street theater performance of the Passion of Christ on the Via Dolorosa in Jerusalem for over thirty years." This pageant has had an immense impact on participants and viewers, as it exemplified for decades Jesus's "redemptive love." Placed as it was in timing and location, it became a central iconic part of Holy Week.

Olga Soler, who is accomplished in many art forms, has been for decades a consummate actress who continues to blend music and pictorial art into her live performances. With her background in professional theater and her enduring commitment to Christ, Olga is the living embodiment of the promise in Joel 2:28. Through the medium of her Estuary Ministries, Olga has ministered for decades bringing thoughtful, Christ-glorifying messages to her many audiences.

Actress Jozy Pollock continued to do street theater a decade after BST on Hollywood Boulevard, encountering a similar kind of hostility, mixed with the power of God's grace in lives changing that underscores the immediacy of street theater to bring out the worst and the best in audiences, caught up themselves in the war against heaven, while at times experiencing the triumph that heaven can bring them through the artistic witness of lives like Jozy's yielded to Jesus Christ.

Singer and composer Sheri Pedigo has been a long-time participant in street ministry, finding a parallel experience to that expressed by Father James Bernstein, as Sheri notes, "It was a powerful experience as the music drew everyone to us." There is, indeed, power in the proclamation of what Jesus has done for humanity if only we allow ourselves to be conduits of God's grace bringing healing of the Spirit to a wounded world, as Sheri is attempting to do.

Perhaps the most direct heir of the legacy of Berkeley Street Theatre is present author JMD Myers, who, in words we can adopt from her chapter, is herself "concerned with social justice, in love with good art," and "speaking challenging messages to [her] culture, not just parroting them back" to herself. A Renaissance woman in her own right, she can write outstanding plays, create and sing beautiful songs to propel them, design and sew

Tamiami Station, Miami, Florida.

striking costumes to display them, is consummate at stage managing them, and has the ability to act in any part and rivet the audience. Jasmine (as we know her), young as she may be at this time of writing, is one of the greats (and, if you haven't had the blessing to see Still Small Theatre Troupe in action—you heard it here first . . . so do so!). I've often told her that she is like Kurt Vonnegut's Billy Pilgrim, unmoored in time as an atavistic throwback to the best days of the Jesus Movement. Her ardency for God is a creative fire that pulses through her art. Her chapter could as easily have been written back in 1971 as today, because the work of Still Small is timeless and its able theater troupe can move easily from its own contemporary classics like *The Diary of Perpetua* and *How We Found Our Father* to their recent performance of *Godspell* at the Salem, MA Old Town Hall, a place she often performed when at Gordon College in the college's participatory theater production of *The Trial of Bridget Bishop*.

As with Still Small Theatre's ministry, today I note the net is filling with innovative Christian playwrights and theater troupes. Cathy Mays, her daughter Janice and son-in-law Martin out of Covenant Life Church in Gaithersburg, Maryland and New York City's Redeemer Presbyterian Church, respectively, have created Christian Theatre Publications (CTP) with innovative plays like "City Rising," "Pilgrim," "Esther." The Ethiopian Christian Drama is another cutting edge dramatic ministry, as are Cypress Christian Troupe, Delta Christian Drama Association, Salemtube Drama, even a Christian Drama School of New Jersey, with its motto: "Acting is Believing," and many more such ministries, actively pounding the boards and, hopefully, still the street for Jesus Christ.

The Play's Still "the Thing"

Hostile Environment: Understanding and Responding to Anti-Christian Bias, by Dr. George Yancey, a professor of sociology at the University of North Texas, is an important book, revealing a level of anti-Christian sentiment— a "Christianaphobia"—not experienced before in the United States at this present level of hostility. The general (though, as we saw, hardly complete) good will the Jesus Movement experienced has long been replaced by a relativistic, pluralistic spirit of the age where any exclusive claims for truth are the target of societal approbation in the present "spirit of the age." Yet, Christians, to remain Christians, cannot abandon the core message of the gospel: that there is only one name by which people are saved (Acts 4:12). If present readers are experiencing the same degree of push-back that we are in New England, it might be helpful to recall that throughout history the play has been a vehicle for insinuating its message past the sentry of vested power and invading the consciousness of the culture, both in fiction and in real life.

Faced with a corrupt and murderous power block, Will Shakespeare's Hamlet observed in Act 3, scene 2, "The play's the thing to catch the conscience of the King." In real life it was a technique the warrior Joab employed to overpower and capture the conscience of the despotic King David in 2 Samuel 14, staging a one-woman, one-act play to convince him to welcome back his son Absalom to his kingdom.

As the corruption and despotism of anti-Christian sentiment dulls the minds of our citizens, this lesson, demonstrated so well by the example of the Berkeley Street Theatre, might be worth remembering as the way to address the increasingly closing ears around us. Perhaps the body of Christ, both in church or, as JMD Myers noted, in its "grassroots/independent/ antiestablishment" form—or ideally both working together as they often did in the Jesus Movement—should revive the medium of guerilla theater. Just as we saw in the streets of Greece, perhaps once again the play may well be the thing to catch the conscience of our culture.

Bibliography

"The Alternative Jesus: Psychedelic Christ." *Time Magazine* (June 21, 1971). content.time. com/time/covers/0,16641,19710621,00.html.

Androcles. "Graham Crusade Freak-Out." *Right On,* 8, n.d.

Benton, Lee. "Lee Benton's CBS studio meetings, guest speaker, Jozy Pollock." Jan 15, 2015. youtube.com/watch? v=EJHNBivDUTE.

Berkeley Street Theater Newsletter, Spring 1975. Self publication.

Bernstein, Father James. *Surprised by Christ: My Journey from Judaism to Orthodoxy.* Chesterton, IN: Conciliar, 2008.

The Boulder Fish, 8, n.d., 1. No masthead or other information included.

Brockett, Oscar. *History of the Theater*, 9th edition. Boston: Allyn & Bacon, 2003.

Carmichael, Ralph. Liner notes for *NATURAL HIGH,* composed and conducted by Ralph Carmichael and Kurt Kaiser. Waco, TX: Light, LS-5558-LP, back cover.

"In Memoriam." *Cornerstone.* Chicago: Jesus People USA, 197, n.d., 3.

DeFazio, Jeanne C., and John P. Lathrop, eds. *Creative Ways to Build Christian Community.* House of Prisca and Aquila Series. Eugene, OR: Wipf and Stock, 2013.

DeFazio., Jeanne C., and William David Spencer, eds. *Redeeming the Screens.* House of Prisca and Aquila Series. Eugene, OR: Wipf and Stock, 2016.

Eskridge, Larry. *God's Forever Family: The Jesus People Movement in America.* New York: Oxford, 2013.

Ellwood, Jr., Robert S. *One Way: The Jesus Movement and Its Meaning.* Englewood Cliffs, NJ: Prentice-Hall, 1973.

Enroth, Ronald E., Edward E. Erickson, Jr., and Breckenridge C. Peters. *The Jesus People: Old-Time Religion in the Age of Aquarius.* Grand Rapids: Eerdmans, 1972.

Excel, Jerry. "Astrology: The Sky Gods." *Right On*, vol. 3, no. 3, issue 28, n.d., 3.

Free Love, vol. 1, no. 1, c. 1971, 23.

Gilinsky, Jaron. "Californians bring Passion to Jerusalem's Old City." Time.com (2008). content.time.com/time/video/player/0,32068,75560426001_1977063,00.html.

Gitlin, Todd. *The Sixties: Years of Hope, Days of Rage.* New York: Bantam, 1987; rev edition 1993.

JSNI, "'Christians' Closed to Jesus News." *Truth: A Jesus Paper.* vol. 2, no. 9. Spokane, WA: Voice of Elijah, September, 1971, 4.

Kang, C. H. and Edith R. Nelson. *The Discovery of Genesis: How the Truths of Genesis Were Found Hidden in the Chinese Language.* St. Louis: Concordia, 1979.

Kelly, Peter. "Two Kinds of Peace." *The Boulder Fish*, issue 9, mid-summer, 1971, 7.

Kozoll, Noelle Aimee. *On Faith Alone: The Jozy Pollock Story.* Feb 25, 2010. youtube.com/ watch? v=auNvGVfes5U.

Bibliography

Kurlansky, Mark. *1968: The Year That Rocked the World*. New York: Random House, 2004.

Jesus People. *The Liberator*. Washington, D.C., 1971, 12-13.

Lewis, C.S. *The Great Divorce*. New York: Harper One, 2015.

————. *Surprised by Joy*. New York: Harcourt Brace, 1955.

Lindley, Mark. "Veteran of Over 200 Trips says 'I had to do something always because I didn't want to be bored . . . '" *Hollywood Free Paper*. vol. 3, issue 17, 1971, 3.

Loudon, Tom. "If Christ Came Back Today." *The Post-American*, 1971.

Miller, Dennis. "A Time to Dance." *Credence*, vol. 1, no. 2. New York: Credence, 1972, 4.

New York Bible Society International. *Great News, Eternal Edition*. New York: NYBSI, 1969, 8.

Patterson, Norma and Bob. "God Uses Women." *The Ichthus*, vol. 2, no. 4. Cherry Hill, NJ: Ichthus, May, 1972, 4.

Pedigo, Sheri. "Jozy Pollock Interview on Clemente Movie, Manson, & Magic." Aug 29, 2013. youtube.com/watch? v=8KhI2Yh3VrE.

Pendergrass, LeaAnn. *Uniting the Nations*. Mar 25, 2015. youtube.com/watch?v=nSFMo AJuPRk.

————. *Uniting the Nations*. Apr 28, 2015. youtube.com/watch?v=_-c7KwkKCRo.

The Post-American. Deerfield, Ill: Voice of the People's Christian Coalition, fall 1971, 1.

Quebedeaux, Richard. *The Young Evangelicals*. New York: Harper & Row, 1974.

Rookmaker, Hans. *The Creative Gift, Essays on Art and the Christian Life*. Crossway Books. Minneapolis: 1981.

Schaeffer, Edith. *The Hidden Art of Homemaking*. Carol Stream, IL: Tyndale House. 1985.

Schaeffer, Francis A. *Arts and the Bible*, Downers Grove, IL: InterVarsity, 2009.

————. *A Christian View of the Bible as Truth*. Minneapolis: Crossway, 1978.

Sparks, Jack. *God's Forever Family*. Grand Rapids: Zondervan, 1974.

Swartz, David R. *Moral Minority: The Evangelical Left in an Age of Conservatism*. Philadelphia: University of Pennsylvania, 2012.

Sweet, Jeffrey. *The Dramatist's Toolkit*. Portsmouth, NH: Heinemann, 1993.

The Holy Bible, New International Version. Grand Rapids: Zondervan House, 1984.

Tonner, Brian. "1200 Celebrate at Festival," vol. 1, no. 1. North Arlington, NJ: KOINONIA, First Presbyterian Church, January 1972, 4.1-2.

Weil, Simone. "Morality and Literature." In *The Simone Weil Reader*. George A. Panichas, ed. Mt. Kisco, NY: Moyer Bell, 1977.

Wenger, Gemma. Beauty for Ashes. "Jeanne DeFazio re: Creative Ways to Build Christian Community." Segment 613, 26 Oct 2015. youtube.com/watch?v=78JbTZEzZc8.